About the authors

Since the early 1990s, Les Snowdon and Maggie Humphreys have been at the forefront of initiatives to promote the benefits of walking for fitness and healthy living. They believe that walking is unique, because it is accessible to just about anyone – and anyone can begin a fitness walking programme simply by walking out of their own front door!

THE PYRAMID PLAN

Walk Out, Work Out, Lose Weight

Les Snowdon & Maggie Humphreys

Hodder & Stoughton

First published in Great Britain in 1996
by Hodder & Stoughton
A division of Hodder Headline PLC

10 9 8 7 6 5 4 3 2 1

British Library Cataloguing in Publication Data
Snowdon, Les
The pyramid plan
1. Physical fitness 2. Health 3. Exercise 4. Diet
I. Title II. Humphreys, Maggie
613.7

ISBN 0 340 65402 3

Typeset by Palimpsest Book Production Limited,
Polmont, Stirlingshire
Printed and bound in Great Britain by
Cox and Wyman Ltd, Reading

Hodder and Stoughton Ltd
A division of Hodder Headline PLC
338 Euston Road
London NW1 3BH

To all those walkers and wayfarers who have lighted the way before us to reveal the magic of the gentle art of walking.

Acknowledgements

With special thanks for the following contributions:

Exercise illustrations devised by Sandra Sheffield, Fitness and Exercise Cert., SKFA; illustrations by Sue Sharples.
All other illustrations by Rodney Paull.

Contents

Part One

△

The Pyramid Plan

1

The Complete Lifestyle Plan for the 90s

It's not the passing years that are a problem – it's a passive lifestyle.

Unfit, lacking in energy, overweight? Stressed-out, sedentary and low in spirit? Finding it difficult to drag yourself out of bed in the morning? Has your get-up-and-go got-up-and-gone? Do you recognise this person? We do. It was us – seven years ago.

Seven years ago we were both overworked, overweight and over-stressed. Like many people, we had a busy lifestyle that was leaving us increasingly tired and dispirited, and our lives were lacking in energy, vitality and joie de vivre.

Why?

Because we had simply begun to slow down. We had become sedentary – we were spending too much time sitting. Although we had been active in earlier years, playing tennis, squash and walking on weekends, over the years we had replaced an active lifestyle with a passive lifestyle – and if we were not careful we knew that we would risk being part of the statistics.

△ The Armchair Killer

To me the outdoors is what you must pass through in order to get to a taxicab.
Fran Lebowitz

Fran Lebowitz' humour may cause us to laugh, but being a couch potato is no laughing matter. A passive lifestyle is now referred to as 'the armchair killer'. Increasing numbers of people are dying each year 'clinging to their armchairs, car seats and office chairs', when all they need to do is become more active.

△   By their mid-40s, more than 40 per cent of men and over 80 per cent of women spend most of their time sitting.

△   Lack of exercise can be as bad for us as smoking 20 cigarettes a day, or having high blood pressure or high levels of cholesterol (British Heart Foundation report).

△   A sedentary lifestyle is considered so bad for us that it is now listed as a major 'risk factor' on a par with cigarette smoking, high blood pressure and high blood cholestrol (American Heart Association).

A Western way of life – a Western lifestyle, whether it be in China, Connecticut or Tunbridge Wells – is continuing to take its toll on our hearts, our minds and our bodies. An inactive lifestyle doubles the chance of having a heart attack. An inactive lifestyle leaves us easy prey to the stresses and strains of modern life. And an inactive lifestyle makes us fat, fatigued and physically unfit.

Statistics show that most of us in the West are either couch potatoes or the latest hybrid variety, mouse potatoes – the new lords of the sedentary jungle. Whereas the couch potato rarely leaves the comfort of his armchair, the mouse potato rarely takes his eyes away from his computer screen, as he sits scanning the 'information superhighway' with a computer mouse. What is everyone looking for? Don't they know that the 'superhighway' is right there outside their own front door – and it's free.

The Allied Dunbar Fitness Survey in 1992 found that 80 per cent of people believe that exercise is good for them. Funny, other statistics show that more than 50 per cent of people don't exercise at all. And can you doubt it when nearly 50 per cent of men and more than 40 per cent of women in Britain are overweight? We fool ourselves into believing that we are fit when the facts are the reverse – many of us are getting fatter, lazier and unhealthier by the year.

We are told that some people are now spending as much as 25 hours a week watching TV, and they don't even get up to change channels any more – the remote control does it all for them. Labour-saving devices which were designed to make our lives easier are robbing us of all those cumulative daily actions which added together used up energy (burnt calories) and helped to keep us fit. Many of us no longer walk to the corner shops – we take the car. And our children are suffering as a result.

△ Kids on the Skids

'Children are becoming less active,' says Dr Kenneth Cooper, president of the Cooper Aerobics Center in the USA. 'They no longer walk or ride bikes to school – and television has given them more attractive opportunities to be sedentary.'

Children, who at one time would walk to school or to their friends' houses, are now routinely ferried around in cars by their parents. And they would rather use public transport than walk anywhere. A survey carried out by the Schools Health Education Unit at Exeter University found that nearly half the girls and one-third of the boys took less exercise than the equivalent of one 10-minute brisk walk a week. And a study in the USA by the Department of Health and Human Services found that 40 per cent of children between the ages of five and eight were shown to exhibit at least one of the following heart disease risk factors: obesity, hypertension, high blood cholesterol. And the reasons given – inactivity and a sedentary lifestyle.

Remember – it's not just the Western world that suffers from the problems of inactivity. It's a Western lifestyle that causes the problem. Members of the Chinese government were alerted a few years ago when they learnt that their one-child-per-couple birth-control policy was producing a

generation of spoilt, overweight youngsters: a whole generation of single children were being mollycoddled by doting
parents and grandparents. Few girls were able to run, and
almost half the boys couldn't manage one chin-up in the gym.
The Chinese government intervened and tubby teenagers
are now having to do physical exercise for the first time in
their lives.

Inactivity is a killer. If we ignore the warning signs and do
nothing to break out of the downward spiral of our inactivity,
it's only a matter of time before many of us pay the price for
our years of easy living.

△ And This Is Where We Came In . . .

We began by telling you that seven years ago we had suc-
cumbed to several years of easy living. We were overweight,
over-stressed, lethargic and lacking in energy. We had begun
to slow down. We had been spending too much time sitting
and not enough time exercising. Of course, we had plenty
of excuses. You probably know them all:

△ We didn't have enough time.

△ We were too busy.

△ We were too tired at the end of the day.

△ We wanted to relax – not exercise.

In fact, we had tried to keep fit – or so we thought. Over
the years we had tried all the exercise fads going. We
both had an exercise bike in the spare room, and most
weekends we walked in the countryside. We tried jogging
– who didn't? And we sustained injuries – who didn't? We
tried cycling, swimming, skipping, callanetics, callisthenics
and calli-you-name-it. We tried them, but gradually we fell
by the wayside. Sound familiar?

The problem was that we had fallen into the fitness trap.
Because we were trying to keep fit, we had convinced ourselves that we *were* keeping fit. And we were overestimating
the amount of time we were actually spending exercising. It's

like the diet trap – overweight people tend to underestimate the amount that they eat. They don't deliberately lie to themselves – they simply don't realise how much they have eaten. An American study discovered that overweight people not only underestimate the amount they eat but they significantly overestimate the amount of exercise they do.

But it's not just overweight people. Most of us tend to overestimate the amount of time and effort we put into getting fit. In our case, no matter what we did, the pounds were piling on and we were not much fitter than when we started. The real problem was that we were not doing enough of the right type of exercise, often enough. We should have been exercising aerobically at least three times a week for a minimum of 20–30 minutes at a time. We thought we were keeping active, but in reality we could still be classified as sedentary, thus inactive. We were not very different from the couch potatoes who did no exercise. Once this truth dawned on us, we decided to do something about it.

△ The Key to Keeping Fitness Fun

I have found that one key to exercise is to find something you enjoy. Ronald Reagan

What we needed was an exercise regime that would keep us fit and burn away those unwanted pounds. Something that actually worked; something that we could keep up year in, year out; and something that was *fun.*

Many of us fail to keep up exercise because we get bored with it and we view exercise as work. Yes, exercise to many people is *work*! Fitness and exercise, diets and weight loss are seen as work. But they don't have to be. The key is to do an exercise you enjoy until it becomes a regular habit which you can keep up week in, week out throughout the year.

That's the key factor in any exercise programme – doing something you enjoy and having some *fun.* For us, that exercise was walking. We were already enthusiastic weekend walkers, so we simply decided to walk more often, for longer, and at a brisker speed. We knew that brisk walking could provide similar aerobic benefits to other exercises such as cycling, running and swimming, so we decided to schedule 'fitness walking' into our daily lives to get fit and burn away the fat.

> *Home is where one starts from.* T.S. Eliot,
> *Four Quartets*

We worked out our own 30-Day Fitness Walking Plan and day one began at our own front door. To succeed with fitness and weight loss, you must have an exercise that's enjoyable and a motivational plan or schedule, and you also need to make it easy at first, so you don't give up after a few days. Having to travel somewhere first, such as a park or the countryside, gives you too many excuses for not having the time. So our 'journey of a thousand miles' began when we laced up our shoes and set out on a jouney which was to change our lives – literally!

That first walk, at a brisker speed than our normal walks, lasted about 20 minutes, and it taught us two things. First, that it really can be that easy to do some aerobic exercise. And second, that with our 30-Day Fitness Walking Plan, we could see ourselves keeping it up.

After two weeks we were beginning to feel the benefits of regular exercise. We felt better, had more energy and vitality, and some of those unwanted pounds were beginning to shift. And we were experiencing a regular 'mood lift' – the feelgood factor – which carried through to the rest of our lives. We had more staying power to cope with stressful situations, and we felt more relaxed and in control of our lives.

We knew, of course, that if we really wanted to see the pounds burn away, we would have to eat more healthily as well as exercising. So we invented our own 'walking diet' – a low-fat, high-fibre, nutritious diet which, combined with walking, would keep us fit and healthy for life.

After 30 days of aerobic walking and cutting down on fatty foods with our walking diet, we had each lost around half a stone in weight. We were then well on the way to reaching our own weight-loss goals – and building a long-term fitness routine into the bargain. And the rest, as they say, is history. To share our fitness success story, we published our 30-Day Fitness Walking Plan as *The Walking Diet*, and it became a worldwide bestseller.

Now, whilst continuing with our full-time careers, we keep up the healthy eating and walk at least 20 miles a week. That's more than 1,000 miles in a year or the equivalent of walking from Land's End to John o'Groats every year. Not bad for an effort which started simply by walking out of our own front doors.

Having successfully used *The Walking Diet* as a long-term maintenance plan for more than five years, we were motivated to add other exercises to our fitness schedule. Cycling and swimming were two aerobic activities that added variety and fun to our exercise workouts, and it was from this experience that we developed the idea of Pyramid Fitness and why we created The Fitness Pyramid (see Figure 1).

△ The Fitness Pyramid

We created The Fitness Pyramid as a motivational aid to offer people of all ages and levels of fitness an opportunity to take part in low-intensity, low-impact exercise, which would help them improve their aerobic fitness gradually without getting injured or bored. The exercises had to be fun to do, and they had to be capable of involving all the family. That's why we chose what we call the big four (Walk Aerobics, Cycling, Swimming, Low-impact Aerobics) as core activities that would appeal to most people.

Walking is the most common exercise activity in Britain. Cycling and swimming are popular activities in all age groups, and aerobics are performed by around three million people, with an emphasis these days on LI (low-impact) aerobics, either in organised classes or at home using an instructional video. All four are low-intensity, low-impact activities which allow you to begin slowly and build up safely to the necessary level for aerobic fitness.

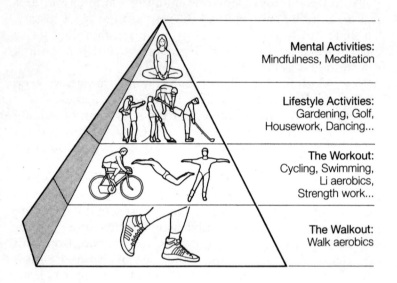

Mental Activities:
Mindfulness, Meditation

Lifestyle Activities:
Gardening, Golf,
Housework, Dancing...

The Workout:
Cycling, Swimming,
Li aerobics,
Strength work...

The Walkout:
Walk aerobics

Figure 1

Pyramid Fitness recognises that everyone is different. Rather than stick to one aerobic activity, you can switch over into other aerobic activities to add variety and give you a break from your usual routine. Of course, you may be quite happy to continue with Walk Aerobics (see page 20) as the mainstay of your long-term maintenance plan. That's fine. This is why Walk Aerobics and The Walkout form the base of The Fitness Pyramid.

The Fitness Pyramid includes aerobic exercise, body conditioning (The Workout), lifestyle activities (gardening, golf, housework, etc.) and mental activities (mindfulness, meditation), and awards space and priority according to their importance within the Pyramid. This, of course, is our Pyramid – yours may be different, as you give priority to other activities within the Pyramid. But more of that later.

The Walkout is the foundation of Pyramid Fitness. It is a low-intensity, low-impact exercise, it's easy and safe, and just about anyone can build up a long-term aerobic habit using it. Since everyone walks, it's simply a matter of walking more often, more briskly and fitting it into your lifestyle. But as your fitness improves using The Walkout, you may wish to move up the Pyramid and try other exercises for variety. For those of you who would like to alternate between at least two types of exercise, then you can mix 'n' match between the other big three workouts on level two of the Pyramid in order to achieve your desired weight loss and fitness.

Using The 30-Day Walkout (see page 41) as your foundation plan, simply choose on which days you would like to substitute your walking workout for another aerobic exercise, such as cycling, swimming or LI aerobics. On these days, you need to ensure that you perform your alternative exercise continuously for at least 20 minutes at an aerobic level (at your target heart rate (see page 53) or rate of perceived exertion (see page 51)).

Moving on, the second level of the Pyramid also includes The Whole Body Workout (see page 83). These exercises supplement your aerobic walkout/workout and can be performed a few times a week to build additional stamina, strength and suppleness. It is particularly important, as you will see, to ensure that you include sufficient body-conditioning/muscle-strengthening exercises in your weekly routine to increase and maintain muscle strength. The average inactive person is losing around half a pound of muscle every year. That means a slower metabolism and an increase in body fat.

You will notice that we have not included jogging or running in our Fitness Pyramid. This is deliberate. We don't wish to upset all you enthusiastic joggers and runners, but the motivating idea behind The Fitness Pyramid was to offer a low-intensity, low-impact, aerobic exercise plan which everyone could do, either alone, or with their partners or families. Jogging and running are, for most people – particularly beginners – high-intensity, high-impact exercises, and there is some risk of over-use injury to feet, knees, ankles and hips. 'Jogging may do wonders for your heart,' says Sarah Key, physiotherapist to Prince Charles, 'but it'll do little for your joints.' Most of us can probably recall friends who have started out enthusiastic joggers only to fall by the wayside, days or weeks later, with an injury. Having said that, if you find jogging or running an injury-free exercise, then by all means include it in your own personal exercise options.

Level three of the Pyramid is lifestyle activities – all those things you do each week which are not aerobic activities or recognised body-conditioning activities, but which contribute to stamina, strength and suppleness and burn calories. The beneficial effects of these activities all add up, and they need to be considered in a total fitness programme.

> *The cure of the part should not be attempted without treatment of the whole. No attempt should be made to cure the body without the soul.* Plato

And finally, at the apex of the Pyramid – mental activities/ mindfulness. Mental fitness and physical fitness are opposite sides of the same coin. Mental activities such as mindfulness, meditation and relaxation – simple techniques available to everyone – round out Pyramid Fitness, making it a whole philosophy of life which can heal the body, mind and soul.

Pyramid Fitness is a moderate programme which is accessible to most people, whatever age and level of fitness. Behavioural and psychological studies show that people keep up moderate exercise programmes longer than routines involving intense gruelling workouts. Studies show that 25 per cent of people starting out on fitness programmes today will give them up within a week. Some 60 per cent of those starting out on jogging programmes will drop out or burn out within three months.

Two studies published in *The Physician* and *Sportsmedicine* in the USA about the damaging effects of high-impact aerobics, found that 76 per cent of aerobics instructors and 43 per cent of their students had sustained injuries from the activity. Their shins were most vulnerable, but calf, lower back, foot, ankle, and knee problems were also reported.

The message is that, unless you're very fit and have gradually built up the ability to perform high-impact exercises, it's much easier to follow a low-impact programme where injury and the likelihood of dropping out are minimised. Let's be honest with ourselves. More than 50 per cent of people do very little exercise. If those people are to seriously get back on their feet and perform regular beneficial aerobic exercise, why make it difficult for them?

△ The Pyramid Diet: Natural Weight Control

'Everyone wants a quick fix to lose weight,' says Janet Polivy, obesity and dieting researcher at the University of Toronto, 'but the truth is, diets won't lead to permanent weight loss.'

Fad diets are not the answer. If they were, why is it that 90–95 per cent of people give up on their diet? Calorie counting, low-carbohydrate and low-protein diets may help you lose weight quickly, but at what cost – bad temper, depression, hunger pangs, fatigue, nausea and loss of muscle tissue essential to your body's health. Fad diets are temporary, unpleasant and often nutritionally unsound. You feel deprived and anxious. Instead of helping you to build healthy habits, they intensify your obsession with food. And they simply don't work!

When you diet without exercising, some of that weight you lose can be your lean body mass, or muscle – not fat – resulting in a lower metabolism. Extreme diets can lead to a 15 per cent drop in your metabolic rate. Your body slows down, enabling you to live on less energy. It thinks it's being starved so it conserves fat – the opposite of what you want. Dieting reduces metabolism which reduces weight loss.

In addition to muscle loss through extreme dieting, the typical inactive person loses an average of 1lb (450g) of muscle every two years, while gaining 3lbs (1.3kg) of fat. Since muscle is the metabolic engine which helps you burn more calories – the more muscle you have the more fat you burn – you can begin to understand why maintaining muscle strength is so important to health and fitness. That's one of the reasons why exercise is the key to weight loss. Exercise builds muscle tissue. And since muscles eat up more calories than body fat, your body burns extra calories 24 hours a day.

Exercise will make your diet more successful. Research shows that people who combine healthy eating with regular exercise are more likely to keep weight off than those who only diet. So the answer is not to diet, but to switch to a healthier lifestyle – regular aerobic exercise, strength-conditioning exercises, and healthy eating.

You will notice as you read through the book that we have not included any weight charts or made any reference to the old buzzwords – 'ideal' and 'goal' weight. We prefer the idea of a person's 'reasonable weight' as the best guide to weight maintenance. Reasonable weight is the weight you can achieve and maintain in the short and long term, and is safer than yo-yo dieting.

A study conducted by Duke University Diet and Fitness Center in the USA found that overweight people who lose only small amounts of weight gained additional lifestyle benefits in areas such as self-confidence, interpersonal relations and mobility. When you're trying to lose weight, it's important to focus on the positive changes in your life and not to get obsessed with the numbers.

It's far better to keep active and lose 1–2 lbs (450–900g) a week on a sensible weight-loss plan which keeps it off, than to lose 4–5 lbs (1.8–2.25kg) a week on a fad diet which makes you hungry, irritable and depressed, and where the weight piles back on later. What you need is to revamp your eating habits, and the way to do this is to follow the example of The Healthy Eating Pyramid.

△ The Healthy Eating Pyramid: Revamp Your Eating Habits

Just as an inactive lifestyle can make you fat, so a diet based on high-fat foods can make you fat. Experts used to tell us that if we consumed 3,500 calories more than our bodies needed, then we would gain 1lb (450g) in weight – whatever the source of the calories. We now know that this is not true. Research confirms that the body makes fat more easily from dietary fat than from carbohydrates. Each fat gram we eat contains nine calories, whereas each carbohydrate gram we eat contains only four calories.

To make matters worse, the body uses more than 25 out of every 100 calories of carbohydrates to break down and digest them, but it uses only three to six calories to internally process 100 calories of fat. In other words, a low-fat diet helps your metabolism, but a high-fat diet slows your metabolism and stores fats. And that's not the whole story. Those fats are also raising your cholesterol level, damaging your blood vessels and can contribute to cancers and other degenerative diseases.

Over the past few years, the world's leading scientists have provided indications as to exactly what should constitute a healthy diet. Their findings are based on observations that the healthiest people in the world follow three basic habits in their eating:

1.   About half their food is complex carbohydrates (CC foods) such as bread, pasta, potatoes, rice and cereals.
2.   They eat at least five portions of fruit and vegetables a day.
3.   They eat very little saturated fat.

From these findings The Healthy Eating Pyramid evolved. To eat healthily and lose weight you need to revamp your eating habits, and The Healthy Eating Pyramid is the way to do this.

The Healthy Eating Pyramid originated in the USA from nutritional guidelines issued by the US Department of Agriculture. The World Health Organisation has published similar research, and the British Government's recommendations for healthy eating are broadly similar. All these agencies recommend that to eat healthily and maintain realistic weight control, you should follow the outlines of The Healthy Eating Pyramid (see Figure 2).

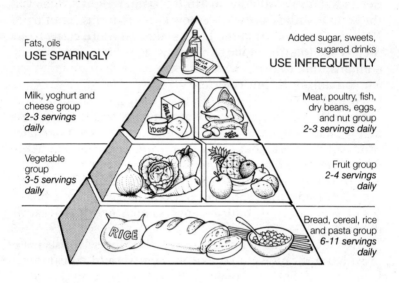

Figure 2

△ One Serving Is . . .

60–75g (2 ½ – 3 oz) lean meat	50g (2 oz) raw vegetables
40–50g (1 ½ – 2 oz) cheese	1 slice bread
50g (2 oz) cooked beans	75g (3 oz) rice, cereal or pasta
150ml (6 fl oz) juice	100–125g (4–5 oz) white fish

From the base to the top of the Pyramid, the main food groups are awarded space according to their contribution to a healthy diet. The Pyramid shows the main food groups at a glance. The foods to increase and give a higher profile in your diet are on the first two levels of the Pyramid – the CC foods (complex carbohydrates such as bread, potatoes, cereals, rice and pasta), fruit and vegetables. These are the foods you should eat most of, so build your meals around them, making CC foods around 50 per cent of your meal, supplemented by generous amounts of fruit and vegetables.

Towards the top of the Pyramid, meat and dairy products play a reducing role in a healthy diet, and fats, oils and sugars should be eaten very sparingly. Remember, it's the fat in your diet that makes you fat, so you should be aiming to cut saturated fat by eating more white meat and fish and using low-fat dairy products. And keep an eye out for 'added' sugar in the form of sugared drinks, cakes, sweets and biscuits. And avoid processed foods, always eating fresh when possible.

Everyone's dietary requirements are different, so you can adapt the guidelines in the Pyramid to match your personal tastes and nutritional needs. It may help to make your diet more interesting by expanding food choices.

To return to CC foods for a moment, a lot of Mediterranean and Far-eastern cooking uses large amounts of fresh fruit and vegetables, with pasta and noodles, plus a relatively small amount of meat. Garnishing CC foods and fresh fruit and vegetables with a smaller amount of meat than usual is the easiest and most nutritious way to improve the quality of your diet and reduce its fat content.

A CC food that is very good for you is bread. Many people still wrongly believe that bread is fattening, and so should be eaten sparingly. In fact, white and brown breads (particularly brown) are low in fat, high in fibre and provide important nutrients our bodies need. Health experts advise eating six slices each day. Bread is the ultimate convenience food: you can eat it anywhere. Instead of eating high-fat snacks, why not try a sandwich made of wholemeal bread with a low-fat filling such as sliced tomato or cucumber with a little reduced-calorie mayonnaise rather than butter.

One slice of bread contains:

△   Complex carbohydrate – a healthy source of energy.

△   Fibre – for efficient digestion.

△   Protein – for growth and repair of body tissues.

△   B vitamins – to help you get the most from your carbohydrates.

△   Iron – for healthy blood and circulation.

△   Calcium – for strong teeth and bones.

Healthy eating habits formed in childhood can remain with us for life. Children who are given nourishing food, such as packed lunches consisting of wholemeal bread sandwiches and fresh fruit, and meals made from fresh, unprocessed foods, are more likely to carry on eating these foods throughout their lives.

By increasing CC foods to around half of your daily calorie intake and eating generous proportions of fruit and vegetables, you will be reducing your dependence on fats, and it will be that much easier to lose weight and to maintain your 'reasonable weight'.

When you follow The Pyramid Plan, you exercise regularly, eat heathily, and let your body reach its 'reasonable weight'. Exercise gets you going, keeps you motivated and gives you more energy. It's then that much easier to keep up healthy eating. And ultimately, you diet not only to lose·weight but to look after your heart and to look after your health. So get off your diet, put away the calorie charts, and start to follow The Pyramid Plan *now!*

△ Why The Pyramid Plan Will Work For You

These are just a few of the benefits you will gain from following The Pyramid Plan.

△ The Walkout

△   The easiest and safest 30-Day aerobic exercise plan.

△   The easiest way for all the family to keep fit.

△   The perfect exercise for weight loss.

△ The Workout

△   Pyramid Fitness adds variety to your workouts.

△ Builds Stamina, Strength and Suppleness – the building blocks of fitness.

△ Builds muscle, helping you to burn more calories.

△ The Weight-off

△ 30-Day Weight-loss Plan helps you walkout, workout and lose weight.

△ Delicious low-fat, high-fibre recipes provide a balanced, nutritious diet.

△ A diet the whole family can follow.

△ The Pyramid Diet Maintenance Plan

△ How to keep up a Pyramid lifestyle.

△ Advice, tips and recipes for lifetime healthy eating.

△ Builds long-term habits that you can keep up for life.

The Pyramid Plan works, and it will work for you, your partner and your family. Discover Pyramid Power and a Pyramid lifestyle today and put some power, energy and vitality back into your life.

2

Walk Aerobics: Today's Smart Exercise

Walk Aerobics is the new aerobics. The most democratic of activities, it's natural, it's easy, it's safe, and just about anyone can do it. Walk Aerobics is brisk, aerobic, fitness walking. A low-intensity, low-impact exercise, it's the foundation exercise in The Pyramid Plan. Since we all walk, it's simply a matter of walking more often and more briskly, and transforming a simple unconscious activity into a meaningful aerobic exercise.

> *It was simply a matter of . . . walking as much as possible.* Hermann Hesse, *A Guest at the Spa*

Walk Aerobics is the opposite of the high-intensity, high-impact 'go for the burn' culture of the 80s – the injuries, the no-pain no-gain, the yo-yo/stop-start treadmill that everyone wanted to be on but couldn't wait to get off. Walk Aerobics is the exercise of the 90s that we can all do without getting injured and burnt out.

So at what point does ambling, strolling, sauntering, etc., become Walk Aerobics? When you walk at a brisk enough pace to give you aerobic benefits.

△ For most people – a pace of 3½ to 4 mph.

△ Walking at your RPE (Rate of Perceived Exertion, see page 51), or walking at your Target Heart Rate (see page 53).

To most people walking is simply a means of getting from point A to point B, but walking can be much more than this routine pedestrian activity. It can be the keystone in an exercise programme which can be built up gradually week by week, without getting injured and without getting bored and fatigued. Without even looking like an exercise, walking produces the same physical fitness, health and weight-control benefits as high-intensity, high-impact exercises, but without the dangers and hazards.

Compared with running (a high-intensity, high-impact exercise), walking produces much less stress on the knee joints – your feet strike the ground with only 1–1½ times body weight when walking compared with three to four times when running. Whereas running mainly builds muscles at the front of the thighs and the back of the calves, walking builds the muscles of the entire leg. From a biomechanical point of view, walking is the easiest and safest aerobic exercise.

△ Why Walk Aerobics Will Work for You

Walking is a very beneficial exercise. Jane Austen, *Pride and Prejudice*

Here are just some of the benefits you will gain from Walk Aerobics (see Figure 3, page 23).

△ Health Benefits

△   Improved heart health.

△   Lower blood pressure.

△   Lower cholesterol – increases 'good cholesterol'.

△   Strengthens bones – helps to prevent osteoporosis.

△   Reduces stress.

△   Improves mood and increases sense of well-being
through release of endorphins (the body's natural
tranquillisers).

△ Weight Loss

△   First-class calorie burning – depletes fat, not muscle.

△   Metabolic rate increased 1–4 hours after walk, assisting further weight loss.

△   May raise resting metabolism – assisting weight loss.

△   Successful long-term weight maintenance.

△ Fitness

△   Increased cardiovascular conditioning.

△   Improved muscle tone and strength.

△ Lifestyle

△   Easiest and safest way for all the family to keep fit.

△   Easiest and safest way for the over 50s to keep fit.

△   Easiest long-term exercise.

△ The Mind, Body, Spirit Connection

The 80s was all about striving for the external things of life
such as money, power and success. The 90s is a time to reflect
and seek more meaning in our lives. The 80s was in favour of
high-impact workouts which burnt many people out. The 90s
is taking a gentler, more moderate approach to exercise and
fitness, with growing interest in 'soft workouts' to physically
and mentally recharge.

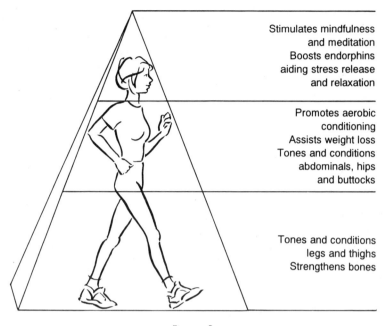

Stimulates mindfulness
and meditation
Boosts endorphins
aiding stress release
and relaxation

Promotes aerobic
conditioning
Assists weight loss
Tones and conditions
abdominals, hips
and buttocks

Tones and conditions
legs and thighs
Strengthens bones

Figure 3

In a 1994 survey in the US magazine *Walking*, 98 per cent of readers said that a primary reason for walking was to feel good afterwards. It seems that many people walk not just for fitness or weight loss, but for the psychological and spiritual benefits and the stress-releasing qualities of exercise.

> *. . . listening to the pulse beat of the earth.*
> Hermann Hesse

Exercise may allow you to touch your toes, but can it touch your soul? The Chinese say that 'the true man breathes with his heels'. Walking allows us to get back in touch with our soul, our spirit, our essence – who we really are. It's a totally natural activity, and it has the ability to make us whole. The Romans believed that the care of the soul was as important as the care of the body.

Walking can give you some space in your life and allow you to feel that you are in control. One of the biggest causes of stress is the feeling that 'we are not in control'. Out there on the open road, you are in control, and the open road can reveal itself as a place of endless wonder and discovery for the true seeker.

As you can see, Walk Aerobics can be much more than simply walking for fitness – it can be a whole philosophy of life.

△ The 10-Minute Walkout

This is where you begin if you're unfit and/or overweight and have been inactive for some time. If you consider yourself reasonably fit and active – if you exercise occasionally, walking, running, aerobics, other sports – then you can move straight to The 7-Day Walkout on page 26.

We're starting to get to know each other now, so let's drop the formalities and just hit the road! Here's how: you simply walk out of your own front door and walk for five minutes along a familiar route at a normal, comfortable speed. Then turn around and come home. It's as simple as that. So no delaying tactics, no excuses. Put this book down and do that 10-minute walk – *now*!

Easy, wasn't it? Well, that was one of the most important decisions you will ever make. You can pat yourself on the back. You're already a winner! You've finished your first 10-Minute Walkout and you should be feeling energised and motivated to continue building up a habit that will help you to get fit and keep healthy for the rest of your life.

And that is what The Pyramid Plan is all about. The 10-Minute Walkout, The 7-Day Walkout and The 30-Day Walkout are all motivational plans to get you started and keep you going. And in keeping going – maintaining the exercise week in, week out throughout the year – is where you will see the real long-term benefits in terms of fitness, health and weight control.

So don't undervalue your 10-Minute Walkout, and don't

think that 10 minutes isn't enough to begin with. It is. That 10-Minute Walkout will have given you a well-deserved workout – a *real* workout. You will have been using the large muscle groups in your legs and arms, and you will have elevated your heart rate sufficiently to give you an increased feeling of well-being. And you will be creating that new exercise habit that you will be able to keep up for the rest of your life.

But remember, take it easy at this stage. If you have been inactive for some time, then you are setting out to regain some of the body suppleness and stamina that you have lost over the years of inactivity. So you need to be gentle with your body. If you treat your body gently at this stage and walk within your own fitness ability, then you will find it easy to build up a fitness routine that you can keep up for the rest of your life. If you are walking with others you should be able to talk easily without getting out of breath, and at the end of your walk you should feel refreshed, not tired and sore.

Although walking is a low-impact, moderate exercise, it is still possible to overdo it. It's so easy to push yourself too hard in the first week, aiming for quick results. The next thing is you're injured – you've strained yourself or pulled a muscle – or you're too tired, too sore or too drained to carry on. Then you're out of action and it makes it that much harder to get your enthusiasm going and begin again. That's when you become just another exercise drop-out. Surveys show that 25 per cent of people who start exercise programmes quit in the first week. So start slowly and do the 10-Minute Walkout. Make sure that you don't increase your speed at this stage, and keep within your own fitness ability at all times. That way you will continue to be a winner.

Now for your second day. You need to walk for another 10 minutes but this time you choose where and when you would like to walk. Perhaps you would like to walk first thing in the morning or fit in a lunchtime walk. Or maybe you'd like to walk after work or late in the evening. Either way, make sure you do your 10-Minute Walkout. You will soon begin to feel the cumulative and habit-forming effects of regular exercise, and you will be raring to get out each day for more. And whatever happens, don't let the weather stop you.

At this stage, you may feel good about your 10-Minute Walkouts. So if you can comfortably do them each day without getting out of breath or tiring yourself, then you have achieved your 10-Minute Walkout goal, and you can move straight on to The 7-Day Walkout. But if you feel that you're not ready to begin increasing the duration of your walks just yet, then continue with 10-Minute walks for another week, maybe even two weeks or more, making sure that you take a rest day every three or four days until you feel confident to tackle the 7-Day Walkout.

△ The 7-Day Walkout

This is where you begin if you consider yourself reasonably fit and active, if you exercise occasionally – walking, running, aerobics or other sports.

The 7-Day Walkout (see Table 1) is designed to ease you gently into brisk, aerobic walking, and to prepare you for the aerobic exertion provided by The 30-Day Walkout. The 7-Day Walkout assumes that you can walk at a comfortable pace for 10 minutes without tiring or getting out of breath – the goal for the 10-Minute Walkout.

So let's step it up a gear! Over seven days you are going to gradually increase your walking time from 10 minutes at a comfortable pace up to 20 minutes at a brisk, aerobic pace at the end of the week. You can follow the lead of The 10-Minute Walkout and just walk out of your own front door along a familiar route and back, or you may want to schedule walks for different times of the day – morning, lunchtime or evening.

Or take a friend with you – a partner, a member of the family or a work colleague – anyone who will help keep you interested and motivated. At this stage you are trying to build a long-term exercise habit, so you can do with all the help you can get.

On the first two days of your 7-Day Walkout, walk at a

	Pace	Time Planned (Mins)	Time Walked (Mins)	Notes: Route, how it felt, weather etc.
Day 1	Moderate	10–15		
Day 2	Moderate	10–15		
Day 3	Moderate to Brisk	15		
Day 4	Moderate to Brisk	15–20		
Day 5	-	Rest		
Day 6	Brisk	15–20		
Day 7	Brisk	20		
Weekly Total				

Table 1

moderate pace for a minimum of 10 and a maximum of 15 minutes each day, building up so that by Day 3 you can step up the pace a little and try a brisker walk for 15 minutes.

What is a brisk pace? At this level, it's a pace which is a little faster and needs a little more exertion than your normal walking pace, let's say walking quickly to catch a bus. We are not going into specific walking speeds at this stage – that can come later. This is your own personal plan so you can pace yourself and decide on a speed that feels comfortable and that doesn't tire you. As you begin to increase speed up to an aerobic pace, you need to warm-up by increasing your pace gradually, and then cool down by reducing your pace gradually for a few minutes towards the end of the walk. This will ensure that your body is prepared for the increased exertion and that it returns gradually to normal after exercise.

If you're walking with a partner take the Talk Test – if you can't hold a conversation without getting out of breath, then you're going too fast. So slow down a little to a pace which is more comfortable. The Talk Test is a good guide at any walking pace, from a moderate to a brisk, aerobic pace, and it will ensure that you never over-exert and injure yourself.

Filling in a walking log each day will help keep you motivated. Fill in the time walked each day, and total the times at the end of the week to see just how well you have done. This is the benefit of recording your walks – you can look back and chart your progress. It's a kind of feedback. Then the more you walk, the more you will want to walk. Make additional notes about the route you take, the 'feelings' you had and the state of the weather. It's fun to write, and it makes interesting reading later. If you really want to go into detailed feelings about your walking day then start a walking journal and record all those special thoughts and feelings along the way.

On Day 4 continue at a moderate to brisk pace, but increase the length of your walk to 15–20 minutes. On Day 5 take a rest. Rest and recovery are an essential part of any exercise programme. Then on Day 6 walk briskly for 15–20 minutes. Continue at your new pace for Day 7, walking for 20 minutes. During your walk, visualise the next 30 days ahead when you are going to be fitter, slimmer and healthier than you have been for a long time.

Well, that's it! Your 7-Day Walkout will hopefully have given you a new perspective, a new sense of purpose and a desire to succeed where previously you have failed. Part of the magic of walking is that the world really does look, smell and feel a different place at three to four miles an hour. Once you get moving and into a routine, just look around you – you might be amazed at what you have been missing. We all do a lot of looking. We look at televisions, videos and computer screens. We look through telescopes and lenses, and we travel abroad to sightsee and experience. And yet, we seem to see less and less and we are often blinkered to what is going on around us on our own doorstep. So step outside, look around you, indulge your senses and just keep walking!

△ On Your Feet

But before you step into your 30-Day Walkout, let's discuss a few ground rules which will help you along the way.

The only equipment you need is a pair of well-cushioned, supportive shoes. As your feet can take 200 tons of weight each day, it seems only fair that you should provide them with a little cushioning. Although you can walk in almost any kind of shoe, you will go further and faster and in more comfort if you wear the right kind. Choose either a training shoe which is specially made for walking or an all purpose 'cross-training' shoe which you can use for walking, running and other sports. There are a number of run-walk shoes now coming on to the market which are designed purely for run-walk fitness programmes. Walking is a cheap and safe way to exercise and keep fit, but it's still important to have the right equipment. If you look after your feet they'll look after you.

The following tips will help you choose the right shoes:

△   Try them on late in the day – your feet tend to swell as the day wears on.

△   Wear socks similar to those you will be walking in – perhaps you like wearing thicker socks.

△   Do they feel flexible – do they support your weight?

△   Is there enough space in the toe-box for you to wiggle your toes? When you push off, your toes will want to expand and spread.

△   Is the heel firm enough? It should be firm but not rigid.

△   Walk around the shop. If they are not comfortable, don't buy them. Don't fall for sales talk that they will wear in and expand – they probably won't.

Although feet are tough, walking on surfaces as different as sand, earth and concrete can take their toll. So let's talk further about how to look after your feet and how to pamper them a little.

Some people don't wear socks, but that's not a good idea either for you or for your shoes. Socks not only protect the feet from injury but they disperse or 'wick away' perspiration which would otherwise eat into the lining of your shoes. Since each foot can sweat as much as a cup of perspiration a day, shoes can be easily damaged, and they can become uncomfortable, causing corns and blisters.

The best socks are those which provide cushioning and which draw perspiration away from your feet, leaving them dry and cool. Cotton alone absorbs moisture whereas blends of synthetics with cotton or all-synthetic socks such as orlon, polypropylene and stretch nylon or a mixture of these, allow the moisture to evaporate. Change your socks every day and, if on long walks your feet perspire a lot, change your socks whenever they get wet. Consider socks that are padded in high-impact areas like the heel and toe and others with additional cushioning on the sole and top of the sock. You really will be 'walking on air'.

△ **The Warm-up**

Your 7-Day Walkout has shown you how to quickly build up a regular routine – to walk for 20 minutes at a time without getting tired or breathless. But before you step up the pace in The 30-Day Walkout and begin The Weight-off, we would like you to do a few simple exercises each day before you walk – The Warm-up – to improve your performance and prevent you getting injured.

As a low-impact exercise which we all do every day to some extent, you may think that performing a warm-up before you walk isn't necessary – but you would be wrong. Warming up raises the pulse, gets the blood flowing, lubricates the joints, and prepares the muscles for more intense activity. Sudden exertion without a gradual warm-up can lead to abnormal heart rate and changes in blood pressure, which can be dangerous, especially for older exercisers.

1 Deep Breathing
To increase oxygen flow/to loosen shoulders and chest
Stand tall, with feet slightly wider than hip width apart, knees slightly bent, abdominals pulled in and pelvis tucked under. Inhale as arms are raised above head and exhale as arms are lowered.

2 Squats

To warm quadriceps/front of thighs
Stand as above, but with feet slightly wider and toes pointing outwards. Slowly bend legs, knees out towards toes, then lengthen legs, keeping knees slightly bent with hips directly under shoulders and back straight. Lower and lift 2 × 8 times.

3 Toe Taps

Transfer weight from one side of body to other and tap right toe on the floor (reach right arm up to ceiling). Repeat with left toe and arm. Alternate from side to side 8 times. Keep back straight, abdominals pulled in and hips tucked under.

4 Hamstring Curl

To increase circulation and warm back of thighs
As above, moving from one foot to the other. Lift right heel back towards right buttock then lower and repeat with left foot. Keep shoulders back and chest up.

5 Marching

To increase blood flow and oxygen uptake to working muscles
March on the spot and swing arms with feet wide for 8 counts then feet narrow for 8 counts. Repeat 3 times. Stay tall with deep steady breathing.

6 Knee Lifts

To raise pulse rate, warm major muscle groups in legs and help to mobilise the back

Walk on the spot, abdominals in and shoulders back. Lift alternate knee up to hip level until parallel to floor. Swing arms back and forth, gradually bringing opposite elbow to knee. Come back to a march and gradually to a walk on the spot.

△ The Quick Stretch

The more you walk and the more briskly you walk, the more likely that the main muscles used in walking could tighten up, so a few simple stretches will loosen them up. The Quick Stretch should only be done when the muscles and tendons are well warmed up. Although you do your warm-up before you walk, you do your Quick Stretch after warm-up exercises

7 Hamstring Stretch

To pre-lengthen and prepare muscles behind thigh

Bend left leg, hands on left thigh. Straighten out right leg in front of you. Point toes, keep knees in line. With a long trunk, lean forward slightly, lifting chest and holding abdominals in (do not bend from the waist). Feel the stretch behind the right thigh in the hamstring muscles as the right leg is lengthened slowly. Hold for 10–15 seconds. Repeat on other leg.

and a few minutes of walking at a moderate pace (prior to brisk, aerobic walking), or you include it in your 'post stretch' when you finish your walk (preferably both times). These exercises stretch the main muscle groups which you use when you walk – the quadriceps (the large muscle group on the front of the thigh), the hamstrings (the back of the thigh) and the calf muscles which are connected to the Achilles tendons.

8 Calf Stretch
To stretch out main body of calf
Bend left knee, keeping it directly over left heel as the right leg is extended back until the right heel is flat to the floor with toes pointing straight ahead. Gently ease chest forward with a straight back bending from the hip. Head up and abdominals in. Repeat on other leg.

9 Quadricep Stretch
Using a chair or the wall for balance, stand on left leg with knee slightly bent, pelvis tucked under, trunk upright. Hold on to right foot. Keep knees together and ease right heel towards right buttock as the right hip extends gently forward.

△ **The Post Stretch**

A cool-down after aerobic walking is as important as a warm-up before you walk. As you come to the end of your walk, gently reduce your pace over several minutes so that your heart and blood pressure can begin returning to normal. Then end your Walkout with The Post Stretch. Repeat stretches 7,8 and 9 above (The Quick Stretch), and add the following stretches to your workout.

As you perform the stretches, aim to progress gradually so that your strength and suppleness improve without straining yourself. The number of repetitions and the length of time for exercises are only a guide – you can reduce them to suit yourself. Always ease into your stretches using smooth, slow movements. If you feel any strain with an exercise, then ease back, go on to another exercise, or leave it out until you feel ready to tackle it again another day. Listen to your body – it is always right.

10 Lower Back

Open feet a little wider than hip width apart, bend knees and place hands on to thighs to support upper body. Pull in abdominals, tuck pelvis underneath and round the lower back. Hold 4 counts. Straighten back and repeat 3 times.

11 Upper Back

Stand with feet apart, knees slightly bent, hips tucked under, abdominals in. Bring hands together in front of chest and press palms forward round upper back and separate shoulder blades. Relax chin down.

12 Chest Stretch

Stand as above, keeping shoulders down and relaxed. Clasp hands behind back. Slowly extend and lengthen arms as they lift up behind back. Hold 4 counts, release and repeat.

13 Shoulder Stretch
Stand as above. Bring right arm across the chest and gently press with opposite hand just above elbow. Hold 4 counts. Repeat other side.

None of the warm-up exercises, or stretches, are compulsory. They are advisable, and should be performed whenever you can find the time to fit them into your schedule. Performing them regularly will lessen the chance of injury and improve your overall performance and enjoyment of walking. However, you should always warm-up and cool-down when performing any exercise, by gradually increasing intensity when you begin, and gradually reducing intensity towards the end of your workout session.

Part Two

Discover Pyramid Power

1

The 30-Day Walkout

The Walkout is the beginning of a journey which will change your life. Like life itself, it will have its ups and downs, but along the way you will discover more about the magic of walking and learn how it can help you get fit, lose weight, and have more energy and vitality than you've ever had before.

Combined with The 30 Day Weight-off, you will be able to get going and keep going, not only for 30 days – but using The Pyramid Maintenance Plan – for the rest of your life. So begin with Day 1 of The Walkout and at the same time start following The 30 Day Weight-off Plan (see page 91).

This is your plan. You are in charge. So step out now and begin making the changes that will lead to a fitter, slimmer, healthier YOU!

DAY 1
STEP IT OUT . . .

The longest journey starts with just one step.
Chinese saying

As you begin your Walkout, the most important consideration is to be clearly aware of your goal ahead – the next 30 days and how you're going to get there. So to help you stay motivated we're going to ask you to keep an exercise log – see FOOTNOTES at the bottom of each page – and to fill it in each day. You will see that we have filled in the TIME PLANNED each day, so today all you have to do is write down WHEN you intend to walk and WHERE. There will be more information about FOOTNOTES in Day 2. Planning in advance of your walk will help you visualise the day ahead and keep your mind on your walking goal. When you know where you are going, it's much easier to get there! So let's move it. Don't forget to warm-up by building your pace gradually at the beginning of your walk and cool-down by gradually decreasing your pace towards the end of the walk.

Footnotes

Time planned (mins): 20–25
Time walked (mins):   a.m.   p.m.
When:
Where:
Comments:

DAY 2
ENERGY BOOSTER: TRY A MORNING WALK

Use morning walks as an energy booster to start the day. Make the morning a quiet time to prepare your mind and body for the day ahead. If you have difficulty making time, try getting up half an hour earlier – the time spent walking will do you more good than the extra sleep or just lying in bed after the alarm has gone off.

You will notice that we have included in FOOTNOTES a blank space for you to fill in, TIME WALKED. When you finish your walk each day you can fill in the time you've *actually* walked compared with your planned walking time. If you get into a good stride and rhythm, you may want to walk further than the time you initially planned. Each day is divided into a.m. and p.m. On the days that you cannot fit in your walk in a single session, then make up the time with two walks to suit your own schedule. It's your schedule. So keep it fun, don't over-exert yourself and keep a log of the extra time you put in – you'll feel really good about yourself when you know that sometimes you are putting in that little bit of extra effort! You can end by making a few brief COMMENTS about your walk – the route you took, your feelings, and the weather. Refer back to page 28 for more information on keeping a walking log.

Footnotes

Time planned (mins): 20–25
Time walked (mins):   a.m.   p.m.
When:
Where:
Comments:

DAY 3
HOW MANY CALORIES WILL I BURN?

A 150lb (68kg) person walking briskly (aerobically) at 3½–4 mph will burn off on average 180–200 calories every 30 minutes. A 200lb (91kg) person walking at the same speed will burn around 235–265 calories every 30 minutes. But to make things easy, let's say that the average person can lose around 100 calories for every 15 minutes of brisk walking. If you add all those calories up each week, that's an awful lot of calories at the end of each month and at the end of the year!

So to help keep you motivated and so that you can see how well you're doing, we're going to ask you to fill in each day how many calories you have burned. No need to be exact. Just do a quick estimate in your mind and keep a cumulative total – add the calories burned each day to the cumulative total from the previous day. That way you can see at a glance how many calories you have burned in a week and at the end of the month.

Footnotes

Time planned (mins): 20–25
Time walked (mins):   a.m.   p.m.
When:
Where:
Comments:

DAY 4
WALK THIS WAY: POSTURE POINTERS

You've heard the saying 'walk tall' – well, today we're going to show you how to become aware of your posture and how to develop a natural walking technique.

The key to a natural technique is to be alert, yet relaxed. Think tall. Imagine a piece of string running upwards through your body and out of the top of your head, reaching for the sky. Then imagine the string pulling you upwards like a puppet. If you think tall, you'll walk tall.

As you walk, keep your back straight, with the weight of your body slightly in front of your ankles. Pull in your stomach and flatten the small of your back by tucking in your buttocks under your spine. Now walk with your head level and eyes focused straight ahead, keeping your shoulders back and down and relaxed. Pulling in your stomach (gently contracting and pressing the abdominal muscles back towards your spine) provides support for your lower back and will help you maintain your most comfortable walking posture.

Footnotes

Time planned (mins): 20–25
Time walked (mins):   a.m.   p.m.
When:
Where:
Comments:

DAY 5
MAKE WALKING PART OF YOUR LIFE

To keep your interest and motivation going, you need to discover new ways to make walking part of your life. So we are now going to show you six creative ways to get the most out of your walks and keep them varied and, above all, *fun*.

△   Walk in the morning – energise yourself for the day ahead (see Day 2).

△   Get off the bus or train one or two stops early or leave your car a distance from your destination and walk the rest of the way.

△   Walk instead of having a coffee break – a walk will give you a better 'lift' than a cup of coffee, and 10 minutes is enough.

△   Try lunchtime walks – invite a friend or start a lunchtime walking group.

△   Walk in the evening to work off your dinner, relax and de-stress.

△   Use weekend walks to visit the country, seaside or some special place.

Footnotes

Time planned (mins): 20–25
Time walked (mins):   a.m.   p.m.
When:
Where:
Comments:

DAY 6
FURTHER POSTURE POINTERS

Today we're going to practise the foot roll and how to walk at an easy, comfortable pace.

As you step from one foot to the other, push off with the ball and toes of your back foot and land in the middle of your front heel. Roll forward through the instep and ball of the foot and push off the toes to take your next step. This motion holds and supports your whole body. You'll be able to walk faster and you'll be more comfortable doing it.

Remember, you're not strolling along watching the world go by! Aerobic walking steps are longer and more purposeful. Take the longest stride that is comfortable, leading with your hips and letting your arms swing naturally in opposition to your legs. Now relax your shoulders, keep them back and down and keep your elbows close in to the side of your body. Your arms will then find their own natural swing and their own natural rhythm.

Footnotes

Time planned (mins): 20 25
Time walked (mins):   a.m.   p.m.
When:
Where:
Comments:

DAY 7
VISUALISATION: THE RIGHT FRAME OF MIND

Most of us visualise all the time, but often in the wrong frame of mind. A negative frame of mind produces negative results; a positive frame of mind produces positive results. Someone going on holiday who is worrying about the weather is already thinking negatively, whereas someone with a positive attitude will probably make the most of their holiday despite the weather.

Scientists tell us that normally we use as little as 10 per cent of our mind's potential. The technique of visualisation allows us to tap into some of that unused potential and focus on specific goals. Visualisation is 'getting the mind to see yourself doing what you want to do'. Sportsmen use visualisation to literally 'see' their desired goal whether it's hitting a ball or winning a race. It's the same with exercise and diet. Each morning visualise yourself walking out, getting fit and losing weight and your positive attitude will help you achieve your goal.

Footnotes

Time planned (mins): 20–25
Time walked (mins): a.m.   p.m.
When:
Where:
Comments:

DAY 8
STEPPING UP A GEAR: INCREASING SPEED

As you begin to step up your speed, you may want to know how fast you're walking. A simple way to measure how fast you're walking is to count how many steps you take per minute. Then using this conversion table (based on an average stride length of 30 inches (75 cm)) you can calculate your speed per hour.

Steps per minute	Minutes per mile	Miles per hour
70	30	2
90	24	2.5
105	20	3
120	17	3.5
140	15	4
160	13	4.5

Footnotes

Time planned (mins): 25–30
Time walked (mins):   a.m.   p.m.
When:
Where:
Comments:

DAY 9
BURN FAT FASTER: THINK OXYGEN

Burning oxygen raises your metabolic rate and burns calories – the more oxygen you breathe the more fat you burn. That's why Walk Aerobics is such an effective way to reduce fat and achieve weight loss. Try these ten ways to burn more oxygen, more calories and more fat.

△   Walking at 3 ½ mph is an effective fat-burning speed.

△   Swing your arms more vigorously.

△   Walk on grass or uneven ground (up to 50 per cent increase in energy expenditure).

△   Get off bus or train one or two stops early – walk rest of way.

△   Leave your car a distance from train station – walk rest of way.

△   Park your car a distance from work – walk rest of way.

△   Climb stairs instead of using lift.

△   Walk to shops if practical instead of taking car.

△   Avoid sitting for long periods – get up and take a walk.

△   Resist using remote controls for the TV and video.

Footnotes

Time planned (mins): 25–30
Time walked (mins):   a.m.   p.m.
When:
Where:
Comments:

DAY 10
MEASURING THE INTENSITY OF
YOUR WORKOUT

One of the easiest ways to gauge the intensity of your workout is to monitor how you feel, your perceived exertion. The Borg scale below relies on your gut sense of how hard you are exercising. It assumes that if you think you are getting a hard workout, then you probably are, and your heart rate is likely to be in the aerobic target zone. As you begin to walk faster, aim for level 4, an intensity which you feel is 'somewhat hard'.

The Borg Scale of Perceived Exertion

0	No Exertion
1	Very Light
2	Fairly Light
3	
4	Somewhat Hard
5	
6	Hard
7	
8	Very Hard
9	
10	Very, Very Hard

Footnotes

Time planned (mins): 25–30
Time walked (mins):   a.m.   p.m.
When:
Where:
Comments:

DAY 11
STAYING FLUID: WHY YOU NEED WATER

Water is the most essential nutrient in your body, and is as necessary to a healthy lifestyle as exercise and a nutritious diet. It's required by all your body's biological functions including the regulation of body temperature and blood volume and the lubrication of joints. Our bodies are between 50 and 70 per cent water and since we lose water through perspiration and breathing and in the elimination of body wastes, we need to replace the loss.

What to do? Don't wait until you're thirsty before drinking water – your thirst always lags behind your body's need for water. By the time you feel thirsty you may have already sweated off about 1 per cent of your body weight, so drink cool water – lots of it – before, during and after exercise. Doctors recommend drinking eight 220 ml (8 fl oz) glasses of water every day.

Although other drinks can contribute to your fluid needs, those containing caffeine or alcohol actually cause you to lose fluid, so stick with your water workout.

Footnotes

Time planned (mins): 25–30
Time walked (mins):   a.m.   p.m.
When:
Where:
Comments:

DAY 12
TARGET HEART RATE (THR) MADE SIMPLE

You must walk vigorously enough to raise your heart beat between 60 per cent and 80 per cent of its maximum. To calculate your THR:

1. Subtract your age from 220. If you're 35, that would be $220 - 35 = 185$.
   That's your maximum heart rate.
2. Now calculate 60 per cent and 80 per cent of your maximum heart rate: $185 \times 0.6 = 111$ and $185 \times 0.8 = 148$.

When walking, your goal is to keep your pulse between 111 and 148 beats per minute. Once into a good walking rhythm, check your pulse at the side of your neck or at your wrist. Using your watch's second hand, count the beats for 6 seconds then multiply by 10 – that's your pulse. If you're outside the lower end of your target range, then speed up – if you're above the higher end, slow down. It's that simple.

Footnotes

Time planned (mins): 25–30
Time walked (mins):   a.m.   p.m.
When:
Where:
Comments:

DAY 13
STEP AWAY FROM STRESS

You know the feeling when everything just gets too much for you – your muscles feel tight, you have a stiff neck and a stiff back, and you end up with a headache or migraine. Feelings of anxiety and tension and, at its worst, depression can build up leaving you with a lack of energy and zest for life. In short – you're stressed out.

To make matters worse, inactivity fuels and adds to the problem. An inactive lifestyle slows down your metabolism so your body burns less calories and you put on weight – and you feel more depressed!

You need to take control of your life and you can start by getting out in the fresh air and going for a walk. Aerobic walking is an instant pick-me-up. Try a 10-Minute Walkout during the day and you will feel the immediate surge of energy recharging you physically and mentally.

Burn out stress before it burns you out.

Footnotes

Time planned (mins): 25–30
Time walked (mins):   a.m.   p.m.
When:
Where:
Comments:

DAY 14
CHANGING THE SCENERY:
WEEKEND WALKS

*One of the pleasantest things in the world is
going on a journey.* William Hazlitt

A weekend walk is a way of getting away from it all, whether
it is to the country, the seaside or perhaps a visit to an historic
town or city where you can combine some sightseeing with
your walking. Whichever option you choose, look upon your
weekend, like Hazlitt, as a journey. Journeys, like holidays,
can be magical. They are a time to let go, relax and take life
as it comes.

To finish your weekend, try dipping into some of the
literature of walking – read Thoreau's essay *Walking*, Leslie
Stephen's *In Praise of Walking* or Charles Dickens' *Night Walks*.
These essays are often included in general books about the
pleasures of walking, available at the library. They provide
motivation and make excellent reading.

Footnotes

Time planned (mins): 25–30
Time walked (mins):   a.m.   p.m.
When:
Where:
Comments:

DAY 15
MOVING ON: BUILDING LONG-TERM HABITS

This week you are stepping up your walks from 30 to 35 minutes. The cumulative benefits of aerobic walking and your Pyramid Diet will be starting to add up – you should have more energy and you should be losing at least 1–2 lbs a week of fat. Not bad for just a few weeks!

Remember to warm-up before and cool-down after your walk. Just a few minutes at the beginning and end of your walk will make all the difference, and ensure that you stay clear of pulled muscles and other injuries. And remember to fill in your walking log. Not only is it a way of congratulating and rewarding yourself, but it builds up a record of achievement over the weeks which you can look back on later. You need all the help you can get when you are trying to build long-term habits. And finally, a reminder to drink plenty of water – keep up those water workouts.

Footnotes

Time planned (mins): 30–35
Time walked (mins):   a.m.   p.m.
When:
Where:
Comments:

DAY 16
LITTLE CHANGES THAT MAKE A
BIG DIFFERENCE

Walking burns calories – lots of them! Take a walking break, walk a mile in 15 minutes and you will burn on average 100 calories (150 lb person). Skip your walk, and you'll be lucky to burn 15 calories. Sit down and eat a small chocolate bar during the same time and you will gain 300 calories. So for a quick pick-me-up that will give you an energy boost and help you cut the calories, take regular walking breaks.

Add one 15-minute walking break to your day, walk a mile and you will burn 36,500 calories in a year. Considering that there are roughly 3,500 calories in 1 lb of stored body fat, that means that you will burn more than 10 lbs of excess fat a year. And that's only exercising 15 minutes extra each day. Cut out that chocolate bar or another 300 calories a day from your diet, and just imagine how many extra calories you could burn in a year. So you see – little changes can make a big difference.

Footnotes

Time planned (mins): 30–35
Time walked (mins):   a.m.   p.m.
When:
Where:
Comments:

DAY 17
PUTTING YOUR HEART INTO IT

A two-year study at the Center for Disease Control in Atlanta, USA, found that the least active people were almost twice as likely to have heart disease as those who were most active. And The British Heart Foundation confirmed this when they reported that lack of exercise can be as bad for us as smoking 20 cigarettes a day, having high levels of blood cholesterol or high blood pressure.

And the easiest way to take exercise?

More than 40 scientific studies have now shown that brisk walking develops cardiovascular health and protects against heart disease. The Paffenburger study in the USA found that walking two miles a day can lower your chance of a heart attack by up to 30 per cent. So to keep your heart in good shape, walk for 30–35 minutes today knowing that you can look forward to a longer, fitter and healthier life.

Footnotes

Time planned (mins): 30–35
Time walked (mins):   a.m.   p.m.
When:
Where:
Comments:

DAY 18
CUTTING THE CHOLESTEROL

Many of us these days are trying to cut down on the fat in our diet. Fat, especially saturated fat, increases the likelihood of heart disease and heart attacks. We are also trying to cut down on cholesterol. Although cholesterol often gets a bad press, it's actually essential to a healthy life. As blood cholesterol, the liver manufactures all the cholesterol your body needs. The real culprit, however, is 'dietary cholesterol'. Cholesterol is found in all animal tissues (including fish and shellfish), in dairy products and offal, and it can cause narrowing of the arteries and heart disease.

What to do? Reduce the amount of fatty foods you eat by following The Pyramid Diet, and exercise. Regular brisk walking lowers blood pressure and raises your HDLs – the so-called 'good cholesterol'. Since stress can also affect your cholesterol level, your 30–35 minute walk today will be helping you relax and keep your cholesterol in check.

Footnotes

Time planned (mins): 30–35
Time walked (mins):   a.m.   p.m.
When:
Where:
Comments:

DAY 19
HOW TO BURN CALORIES QUICKER

To burn away those unwanted pounds quicker, try the following three calorie burners.

△   Walk faster. A 150 lb person burns 300 calories an hour at 3 mph, 370 calories at 3½ mph and 400 calories at 4 mph. But be careful – 3½ mph is a good fat-burning speed for most people, and it's easy to keep up day in, day out. Try faster speeds, but don't push too hard – if you get sore, ease back to a comfortable speed. You may burn more calories by walking longer rather than harder.

△   Walk up hills and increase your level of cardiovascular fitness and burn more calories in less time. On a 5 per cent gradient, walking at 4 mph, you will burn 50 per cent more calories; on a 10 per cent gradient you will burn 100 per cent more calories.

△   Walk after meals at a moderate pace. It helps digestion, increases energy, relieves that bloated feeling – and it burns a few dozen extra calories. They all add up at the end of the day.

Footnotes

Time planned (mins): 30–35
Time walked (mins):   a.m.   p.m.
When:
Where:
Comments:

DAY 20
THREE MORE SUPER CALORIE BURNERS

Add the following to your routine and build long-term habits which you can keep up for the rest of your life.

△　Follow The Whole Body Workout twice a week (see page 83). Resistance training builds more muscle and helps speed up your metabolic engine – and it continues to build more energy for four to six hours afterwards. This can result in an extra 4–5 lbs weight loss in a year.

△　Eat more complex carbohydrates. Cut down on fat by increasing your intake of fruit, vegetables, cereals, grains, pasta and low-fat dairy products. Remember, each fat gram contains nine calories but each carbo calorie contains only four calories.

△　Change your attitude. Looking beyond The 30-Day Walkout, fitness, health and weight loss have to form part of a life-time love affair. So have fun building small habits which you will enjoy keeping up. A positive attitude can burn more calories than all the diets in the world put together.

Footnotes

Time planned (mins): 30–35
Time walked (mins):　a.m.　　　　　　p.m.
When:
Where:
Comments:

DAY 21
ONLY TEN DAYS FROM NOW!

After three weeks, you should really be feeling the benefits of regular aerobic walks and those stubborn pounds should be starting to drop off, never to return. This week, vary your routine to boost your motivation and clock up those extra fat-busting miles. Try walking breaks instead of coffee breaks, or do a 15-minute mile in your lunch hour. Your energy level will soar for the afternoon.

Cultivate awareness. Savour the sights and sounds of your walks, and open your eyes to the world around you. The world at 3½ mph looks a far different place than the world seen from a motor car or train. And cultivate mindfulness. Try a little 'walking meditation'. Walking meditation can give you a feeling of joy, balance and peace. The perfect way to spend part of your lunch hour or some time after work. Or a relaxing way to get out over the weekend. Just 10 more days now to that slimmer, fitter, healthier you!

Footnotes

Time planned (mins): 30–35
Time walked (mins):   a.m.   p.m.
When:
Where:
Comments:

DAY 22
MUSIC WHILE YOU WALK

Walking doesn't have to be a solo performance. Try taking a band or an orchestra with you when you walk. The rhythm of the music will help you maintain a brisk pace. Take a Walkman cassette player/radio with you and listen to your favourite music or listen to one of the specialist walking tapes which gradually increase pace to the beat of the music. Tapes are available which cater for a wide range of musical tastes – pop, classical, country, swing and marches.

Music can do so much for you physically and emotionally. It can help you relax and let go of the damaging effects of tension, anxiety and stress. And it can produce feelings of exhilaration and well-being – an instant high.

A word of warning! Headphones can distract you from traffic or other dangers on the road, so if you listen to music while you walk, remember to look where you are going.

Footnotes

Time planned (mins): 35–40
Time walked (mins):   a.m.   p.m.
When:
Where:
Comments:

DAY 23
WALKING WITH THE WEATHER

Don't use the weather as an excuse to stop you walking. There are few days in the year when the weather is either so hot or so cold that it makes getting outside unpleasant. And even on rainy days, it doesn't often rain the whole day. Simply dress for the weather and pick the best time for your walk.

On cold days, make sure that your extremities are warm – cover your head and neck, wear gloves and make sure that your thighs are kept warm. When the extremities are warm, the whole body can be kept warm with relatively light protection. Don't make the mistake of wearing too many sweaters. Wear several light layers of clothing that can easily be added or removed while you walk. For warm-weather walking, wear light-coloured clothes to reflect heat and light, and wear a brimmed hat when walking in the sun. Walking with the seasons, you can experience the different sensual delights of mist, snow, spring rain and summer showers.

Footnotes

Time planned (mins): 35–40
Time walked (mins):   a.m.   p.m.
When:
Where:
Comments:

DAY 24
WALK-TALK: THERAPY ON THE MOVE

Aerobic exercise has the power to calm jangled nerves and reverse negative moods. Research shows that a 20–30 minute brisk walk can have the same effect as a mild tranquilliser, and it can enhance self-esteem and reduce depression. Walking works the large muscle groups, which can help to release chemicals called endorphins, the body's natural tranquillisers. And the healing power of rhythm unlocks destructive emotions and helps us to relax and let go.

Add to this, the benefits of Walk-Talk therapy. Take a friend, your partner, even include the kids in your walk – and talk. Walking is one of the few exercises that allows you to concentrate as much on each other as the exercise. The walk, the fresh air and the company provides circumstances favourable for listening, talking and discussing vexing problems. Walking together helps you talk together, and helps disperse anxieties and tensions before they become problems. Walking can be powerful therapy.

Footnotes

Time planned (mins): 40
Time walked (mins):   a.m.   p.m.
When:
Where:
Comments:

DAY 25
KEEPING IT UP: MAINTAINING THE MOMENTUM

As you're nearing the end of your 30-Day Walkout, you may have missed an odd day. This won't make much difference, but if you leave more than three days between walking sessions, any gains will be cancelled out. You should also be aware of the long- and short-term effects of starting any exercise programme, then stopping it.

'The easiest way to change yourself is physically . . . physical change is quick,' says American fitness philosopher, Dr George Sheehan. 'If you set your mind to it, in three months you're almost an athlete.' It's true – but it's equally true that if you stop exercising you can lose all the gains in the same time. In the short term, cardiovascular fitness (heart health) develops quickly and deteriorates quickly, whereas muscular strength and endurance can last for up to four weeks after first building up your strength. Hard-won gains in health, fitness, increased energy and weight loss can so easily be cancelled out if you let your exercise programme lapse, thinking that you will pick it up again at a later date. So keep it up and don't lose it – use it.

Footnotes

Time planned (mins): 40–45
Time walked (mins):   a.m.   p.m.
When:
Where:
Comments:

DAY 26
YOU'RE IN GOOD COMPANY:
FAMOUS WALKERS

Hippocrates, the ancient Greek physician known as the Father of Medicine, prescribed early-morning walks, after-dinner walks and night walks. Aristotle, the Greek philosopher, discoursed with his students whilst walking and founded the Peripatetic School of Philosophy.

In the nineteenth century, the high priest of walking was the poet, William Wordsworth. It has been estimated that during the course of his life he walked 185,000 miles in the English Lake District. It was during a walk with Wordsworth that another poet, Coleridge, was given the inspiration for *The Rime of the Ancient Mariner.* He said of walking: 'Such blessing is there in perfect liberty.' Ralph Waldo Emerson, Jane Austen, Walt Whitman, Charles Dickens, Henry David Thoreau and Robert Louis Stevenson were all great walkers, as were Albert Einstein, Bertrand Russell and the American President, Harry S. Truman.

Footnotes

Time planned (mins): 40–45
Time walked (mins):   a.m.   p.m.
When:
Where:
Comments:

DAY 27
BODY AND SOUL: ONLY CONNECT

Walk Aerobics can be much more than just walking for fitness and weight loss. Inner walking can be a way 'to connect' with the deeper reality that we call 'soul' or 'spirit' – a way to feel not only the beating of our own pulse but the pulse of the wind and the pulse of nature and everything around us. It's said that the difference between a good walker and a bad one is that one walks with his heart and the other with his feet. So try 'inner walking'. Get into a comfortable rhythm, then let the distractions within your mind 'go' and sample the meditative benefits of walking.

How does it work? It's something to do with the sense of freedom experienced through the leg muscles – the rhythmic to and fro of the legs, the measured beat of the right foot alternating with the left. The ground can seem almost to be alive, and our senses can become sharper and more focused.

Footnotes

Time planned (mins): 45
Time walked (mins):   a.m.   p.m.
When:
Where:
Comments:

DAY 28
WALK AWAY YOUR PROBLEMS

Ambulando cogitans and *ambulando solvitor* are commonly used Latin phrases which simply mean that walking is good for thinking and for solving problems. Why should walking stimulate thinking? And how can walking seemingly resolve complex problems in a way that thinking sitting down can't? Put simply – the fastest way to relax and still the mind is to move the body. Action absorbs anxiety. Action frees us from the confusion of our conscious thoughts and opens our mind to the freedom of the intuitive, creative mind – the real problem solver.

Try 'the thinking walk'. Whenever your mind is troubled and confused, get into a good walking rhythm, and tap into the limitless creative possibilities of your intuitive mind. Don't force anything – just relax and let your troubles drain away, and you will be surprised how solutions to the most difficult problems just 'drop into your mind', seemingly from nowhere. Eureka!

Or try 'the non-thinking walk'. With this simple Zen method you start by thinking about your problem; then forget it; then wait. In this 'non forcing' space the solution will come without you having to worry about it.

Footnotes

Time planned (mins): rest
Time walked (mins):   a.m   p.m.
When:
Where:
Comments:

DAY 29
EASY SPIRIT: RECORD YOUR FEELINGS

All walking is discovery. On foot we take the time to see things whole. Hal Borland

We all need to find some space just to be ourselves and connect with the deeper reality within us. Inner walking can be the way to make this connection and keeping an 'inner walking diary' can be a fun, creative way to record our thoughts and feelings.

It need take only a few minutes a day to jot down all those special moments that hold meaning for you – sights, sounds, sensations, thoughts. Days, maybe weeks later, you will be surprised to find patterns emerging through your writings. Try making a poem or a collage out of them. You will be amazed what you discover.

Each moment is something very special. It speaks to us personally if we will only listen. Inner walking and an inner walking diary can be a way of constantly rediscovering these special moments.

Footnotes

Time planned (mins): 45
Time walked (mins):   a.m.   p.m.
When:
Where:
Comments:

DAY 30
THE FINAL DAY: CONGRATULATIONS, YOU'VE MADE IT!

Well done – that's a real breakthrough. Not only should you be fitter, slimmer and more energetic, but you should be feeling very pleased with yourself. This was the first month of the rest of your life. You have taken the first steps to develop an exercise routine which you can adapt to your lifestyle and turn into a long-term habit.

It may take longer than 30 days to achieve your desired weight, but you should be well on the way and you now know that you can do it! Keep up the walking, mix 'n' match with other exercises for variety, and keep following the example of The Healthy Eating Pyramid and The Pyramid Diet Maintenance Plan. You will be tougher mentally and nothing will be able to keep you from getting out into the open air. You are in control. It's your plan. So make it work for you.

Footnotes

Time planned (mins): 45
Time walked (mins):   a.m.   p.m.
When:
Where:
Comments:

2

The Workout: Exercising Your Options

Pyramid Fitness recognises that everyone is different. Rather than stick to one aerobic activity, you can switch over into other aerobic activities to add variety and give you a break from your usual routine. Of course, you may be quite happy to continue with your Walkout as the mainstay of your long-term maintenance plan. That's fine. This is why Walk Aerobics forms the base of The Fitness Pyramid. Combine your Walkout with two weekly sessions of The Whole Body Workout on page 83, and Walk Aerobics will give you all the aerobic and body conditioning benefits of the other big three aerobic exercises – cycling, swimming and LI (low-impact) aerobics.

The Walkout is the foundation of Pyramid Fitness (see Figure 4). It is a low-intensity, low-impact exercise, it's easy and safe and just about anyone can build up a long-term aerobic habit using it. Since everyone walks, it's simply a matter of walking more often, more briskly and fitting it into your lifestyle. But as your fitness improves using The Walkout, you may wish to move up the Pyramid and try other exercises for variety. For those of you who would like to alternate between at least two types of exercise, then mix 'n' match between the other big three workouts in order to achieve your desired weight loss and fitness.

Some of you may wish to place more emphasis on one exercise rather than another, so choose cycling, swimming or LI aerobics to supplement The Walkout and to meet your own fitness goals. Or you may, for instance, want to

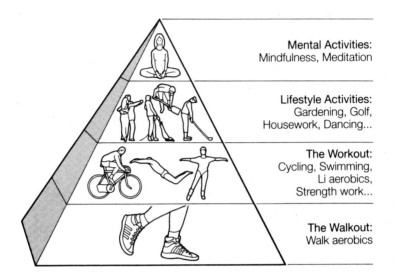

Mental Activities:
Mindfulness, Meditation

Lifestyle Activities:
Gardening, Golf,
Housework, Dancing...

The Workout:
Cycling, Swimming,
Li aerobics,
Strength work...

The Walkout:
Walk aerobics

Figure 4

cycle to work, walk during some lunch hours with a friend, and swim with the family on a weekend. Or perhaps fit in an early-morning swim before work, alternate weekday walks with a LI aerobics class or a fitness video at home, and mix it up on a weekend between all four exercises.

Pyramid Fitness is a form of cross-training, which means that instead of sticking to one activity, you 'cross over' and include several others in your schedule. Cross-training in several activities can give you increased fitness benefits and better overall conditioning than simply sticking with one activity.

Each activity conditions different muscle groups as well as exercising the same muscles in different ways, and it reduces the chance of suffering pulled muscles or other injuries. Each activity complements the others in building overall stamina, strength and suppleness, and is the key to keeping fitness fun.

△ Towards Total Fitness: Stamina, Strength, Suppleness

Only when you can be pliable and soft, can you be hard and strong. Zen proverb

What is fitness? Fitness gives you the vigour and alertness to carry out your daily tasks without undue fatigue, and it leaves you with sufficient energy to enjoy leisure-time pursuits and cope with the unforeseen stresses and strains of living. In other words, being fit lets you do the things you want to do, when you want to do them. Fitness is the goal, but exercise is the way to get there. Fitness consists of three elements.

△ Stamina

Stamina – endurance or aerobic fitness – is the ability to keep going without becoming too tired. Aerobic fitness allows you to breathe more deeply. It increases the efficiency of your heart, lungs, blood and blood vessels, and your muscles become more efficient at using oxygen. Your heart becomes stronger and more efficient, and the effects of aerobic training produce an overall improvement in health and well-being.

△ Strength

Strength is built by pushing muscles repeatedly against a resistance. Stronger muscles enable you to lift and carry with greater ease, and they give you the ability to sustain prolonged activity without getting tired. Stronger muscles are also better shaped and more defined, and can improve posture and physical appearance. After the age of 20, the average person loses approximately 1lb (450g) of muscle every two years if no strength training is done. You either use it or lose it.

△ Suppleness

Also called flexibility, suppleness is the ability of the joints to move through their full potential range of movement. It's your ability to reach, bend, twist and turn without damaging yourself. Suppleness protects the muscles against pulls and tears, since short, tight muscles can more easily be overstretched. Supple muscles and joints also contribute to improved posture and physical appearance.

△ Workout 1   Walk Aerobics

Walk Aerobics is great for stamina building, but for additional strength and suppleness you should perform The Whole Body Workout twice a week. Walking works out almost every one of your body's large muscles, toning and strengthening your hips, thighs, stomach and buttocks, and some of your shoulder muscles when you swing your arms. Adding hill walks to your workouts will improve your cardiovascular health (stamina) and strength (see Day 19, 30-Day Walkout). As a low-risk exercise, Walk Aerobics is the easiest and quickest way to begin a stamina, strength and suppleness programme.

△ Workout 2   Cycling

Cycling is good for stamina building and strength but it won't do as much for your suppleness as swimming or low-impact aerobics. Cycling builds strong upper and lower leg muscles and gives the circulatory system an outstanding aerobic workout. Cycling does, however, help stretch your lower back, conditioning it for other exercises, but you will need to develop your suppleness by following The Whole Body Workout.

If you're a beginner, familiarise yourself with cycling by riding on relatively flat terrain for 20–30 minutes at a time and avoid the most common mistake that novice cyclists make – pedalling in too high a gear. This will wear you out quickly and put undue strain on your knees. Once you're comfortable cycling on level ground, try climbing modest hills, graduating to steeper hills later. When you climb hills, you need to do a lot of work against gravity and this increases the aerobic training effect and brings different muscles into play. Remember to wear a helmet for safety.

△ Workout 3   Swimming

Swimming is excellent for stamina, strength and suppleness, using nearly all the major muscle groups. It works out more than two-thirds of the body's total muscle mass, and so it places a vigorous demand on the heart and lungs, making it one of the very best aerobic exercises. The driving force of swimming is powered by the muscles of the upper body. Swimming helps develop both upper and lower body more uniformly than cycling or low-impact aerobics.

Swimming is the safest endurance activity because you perform it in the cushioning environment of water. Because you swim against water resistance rather than against gravity, the risk of injury to body muscles and joints is low. And it's especially good if you're overweight or have any backache, stiffness or disability.

The aerobic value of swimming depends on how hard you work. Aim to swim continuously for at least 20 minutes. If you are a beginner or haven't visited the pool for some time, then start by swimming the width of the pool, resting between widths. When you can do this easily, try swimming the length of the pool, resting between lengths, then gradually add laps and decrease rest intervals until you can swim continuously for at least 20 minutes. If you are in any doubt as to your ability to swim, then take advice from a trained instructor.

△ Workout 4   Low-impact Aerobics

Low-impact aerobics is a continuous exercise routine where one foot is always in contact with the ground – squats, knee lifts, lunges, etc. This reduces the risk of potential injury caused by repetitive, high-impact (hopping or jumping) movements. A typical low-impact routine to music uses the large muscle groups in the upper and lower body and has benefits such as increased stamina, strength and suppleness and improved circulation and body-fat reduction.

LI aerobics is suitable for all fitness levels – beginners, older participants, the overweight and unfit – and is best performed in a class with a trained instructor. Before you join a class, consider what you want to achieve, and ask the instructor if you'll be able to do it, making sure that the level is right for you. Joining a class that is too difficult will only leave you feeling exhausted and you may not want to go again. As with all exercise, build up intensity gradually and listen to how your body feels. It's always right. That way you won't injure yourself. If you want to exercise at home, try a low-impact aerobics instructional video.

△ **Five Steps to Fitness**

The following five steps will get you going along the road to exercising your options:

△ Step 1   Select Your Activities

Remember – you're setting out to have some fun and enjoy yourself, so choose activities which you can keep up and develop into long-term habits. When you enjoy yourself, your body is more relaxed, and you get the most out of your exercise sessions. Experiment with different activities. If you haven't been to the swimming pool for years or been on a bicycle, give it a whirl. If you don't have a bicycle, you don't have to dash out and buy one. They can usually be hired quite cheaply if you want to try out the experience. Try all four exercises – walk aerobics, cycling, swimming, low-impact aerobics – and mix 'n' match until you find the balance that suits you. After all, this is what Pyramid Fitness is all about – creating your own personalised fitness programme.

It is what makes The Pyramid Plan unique. It's completely versatile and it works just for you, to suit your needs and your fitness, health and weight-loss goals. For extra motivation, why not involve your family and friends. If they can't go with you, then discuss with them how important it is to you to have this time for yourself during the week.

△ Step 2   Make an Exercise Schedule

When you have selected your activities, you will need to decide when to fit them into your schedule. A schedule will help you to avoid common excuses such as, 'I haven't got the time to exercise.' Don't forget that getting started is actually as simple as stepping outside for a walk around the block. If you experience difficulties slotting in some activities because of changing plans, you can always use walking as a workout to get you out of trouble. Consider walking to your next appointment or breaking up your workouts into shorter sessions – two 15-minute sessions. Even if you have a busy life, a little forward planning will help you slot workouts into your day. Figure 5 is a sample of an exercise schedule to give you some ideas for creating your own. Experiment with the following time slots:

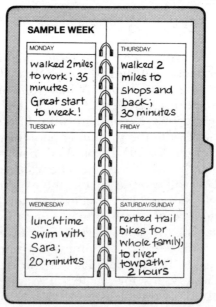

SAMPLE WEEK

MONDAY

walked 2 miles to work; 35 minutes. Great start to week!

TUESDAY

WEDNESDAY

lunchtime swim with Sara; 20 minutes

THURSDAY

walked 2 miles to shops and back; 30 minutes

FRIDAY

SATURDAY/SUNDAY

rented trail bikes for whole family; to river towpath – 2 hours

Figure 5

MORNING   If you're an early bird, the morning may be the best time for you to go for a walk, swim or bike ride. Morning workouts energise you and give you space to plan the day ahead. If you would rather turn over in bed than face a 'rise and shine workout', then try putting the alarm on half an hour earlier. The early start may be more beneficial than the extra time in bed.

LUNCH HOUR   Re-charge yourself for the afternoon. A brisk 30-minute walk will lift drooping energy levels and power your body for the rest of the day. Take a friend or friends – start a lunchtime walking club. It doesn't have to be every day – two 30-minute lunchtime walks each week will burn around 400 calories and, combined with a light Pyramid Diet lunch, will help to keep you trim and fit. Or try a lunchtime swim.

AFTER WORK   For many people this will be the most convenient time of day to workout. It can also be a time for more excuses – 'I'm tired,' 'I'd rather have a drink with friends,' and another hundred and one reasons for avoiding the effort. Yet, if you make the effort, you will soon discover that exercise gives you a 'second wind' and re-charges you for the evening. The evening is probably the best time for most people to attend an LI aerobics class, but if you just want an easy way to relax away the day's problems, then take a brisk 30-minute walk.

COMMUTING TO WORK   If it's convenient, walk or cycle to work, at least a few days each week. If your workplace is too far, walk or cycle to the bus or train station or try getting off the bus or train one or two stops earlier on your way to work or returning home from work and walk the rest of the way. One of the best ways to stay motivated is to tie up with some friends and fellow commuters whose schedule matches yours.

THE WEEKEND   This may be a good time to spend some quality time with a friend, a partner, or plan a family activity.

Be creative. Plan your workouts around other activities – visiting the countryside, seaside or a surprise destination. If you have a busy week ahead, planning workouts for both Saturday and Sunday may free up time during the week. Alternatively, take your rest day over the weekend. Rest and recovery are important elements of health and fitness.

THE FLEXITIME WORKOUT   For those of you who don't keep standard working hours. You may have the whole day to exercise in, or have certain times of the day which are better for you than others. Either way, choose the times that are most effective and give the best results. Exercising at the same time each day will put you in an 'exercise mood' and help you build long-term habits.

△ Step 3   Go For It!

As with all aerobic exercises, your goal is to reach a level of exertion that causes your heart to pump for a minimum of 20–30 minutes at your target heart rate – the optimal rate for burning fat, losing weight and maintaining a healthy heart. A well-balanced exercise programme includes at least three to five weekly sessions of cardiovascular (aerobic) exercise plus two sessions of body conditioning, The Whole Body Workout (see page 83). So aim to exercise for at least 20 minutes without stopping, although if you have been inactive for some time, make this your goal, and work up to it gradually. Remember always to perform The Warm-up, The Quick Stretch and Post Stretch as necessary (see pages 31–38). Low-impact aerobic classes should include their own.

Measure your target heart rate by following the advice on page 53 (Target Heart Rate Made Simple) or alternatively use the Borg Scale: Rate of Perceived Exertion on page 51 to monitor your exercise intensity. Another simple way is to use the 'Talk Test' as a benchmark to ensure that you are not working at too high a level – you should be able to carry on a normal conversation without getting out of breath (see page 28).

▲ Step 4   Aerobic and Lifestyle Activities: All Calories Count

Aerobic Activities	*Calories Burned in 1 Hour*
Walk Aerobics – 4 mph	400
Cycling – 10 mph	420
Swimming – slow crawl	520
– slow breast stroke	540
Low-impact Aerobics	360
Stationary Bicycle – 10 mph	430

Lifestyle activities may not have the same cardiovascular conditioning effect as the aerobic exercises above, but they are all helpful in keeping your heart healthy. And they contribute to weight loss. Don't forget that all calories count – even the non-aerobic ones! The average game of golf, carrying your own clubs, burns around 325 calories an hour. Gardening – weeding, trimming and raking – can burn about 300 calories an hour; pushing a manual lawn mower burns between 420 and 480 calories an hour (as many as an hour of tennis). Housework – scrubbing, mopping and window cleaning without pause – can rack up 250 calories an hour, while washing clothes can soak you for 160 calories an hour. Think of all the activities you could add to your daily life that would increase your activity and help burn calories. You need to work at a constant pace and – as with any kind of exercise – you need to warm-up and stretch before you start (see page 31).

The above figures are estimates based on a 150 lb (68kg) person, but the actual number of calories burned varies with age, fitness level, calorie intake and metabolic rate. Calories will continue to be burned at an accelerated rate for several hours after the workout.

△ Step 5   Mental Activities: Mindfulness and Meditation

Going is important – not arriving.
Thich Nhat Hanh

Mental activities – mindfulness and meditation – form the apex of The Fitness Pyramid. Mental fitness and physical fitness are inseparable. A sound mind in a sound body was an ideal valued by the Romans and Ancient Greeks. To achieve physical fitness, we push ourselves harder – to achieve mental fitness, we simply let go and relax.

Mindfulness – mindful awareness – is a gentle way of looking at the world. Mindfulness allows you to connect with your 'inner self'. Mindfulness is walking meditation. It can bring you feelings of joy, balance and peace while you practise it. You start by walking at a comfortable, relaxing pace, while breathing normally. Then after a few minutes you begin to pay attention to how many steps you are taking. It is by concentrating on 'one point' – one thing at a time – that the mind is stilled and centred. It is this mindful attention and awareness that releases your energy, vitality and creativity. It can be a cathartic experience, freeing you from the anxieties and fears of the everyday world.

Counting steps is one meditation – movement meditation is another. Feel the spring of your heel and toes as they make contact with the ground, and sense literally being 'grounded' in the earth and Nature. We quoted earlier the Chinese sage who said that 'the true man breathes with his heels'. Stay with these feelings in mindful awareness and get to know them.

Another meditation you can try is counting your breath. Counting breaths is making contact with the basic rhythm of life – inhalation and exhalation is like the ebb and flow of the oceans and the movement of the planets. As you walk, count your exhalations up to four and begin again, or choose another number which you feel comfortable with. Or pick out a distant object on your path and count your breaths until you get there.

The fastest way to still the mind is to move the body. Feelings and creative thoughts come to the mind a lot more easily while participating in exercise involving the rhythmic flow of the body, such as walking. Most people report an immediate boost of spirit after walking meditation – like a 'mind massage', an awakening of the senses, and a realisation of living in the moment. So give yourself a 'mind massage' and try walking meditation.

Mindfulness and walking meditation round out Pyramid Fitness, making it a whole philosophy of life which can heal the body, mind and soul.

△ The Whole Body Workout

Through the years, everyone loses muscle (about 5 lbs (2.25 kg) per decade) and gains fat (about 15 lbs (6.75 kg) per decade), says American exercise expert, Wayne Westcott. 'To reverse these processes, you need to develop a sensible programme of strength training to boost your muscle tissue and metabolic rate, and a regular programme of endurance exercises to decrease your fat stores.' So you exercise aerobically to burn fat and you do strength training to build the muscle that keeps it from returning.

When your muscle mass decreases, your metabolism slows down, so more calories are stored as fat than burned as fuel. That's bad news for those trying to lose weight or trying to keep the pounds from creeping on. Your muscles are your metabolic engine and you need strong ones to perform physical activity. Losing muscle is like going from a six- to a four- to a two-cylinder car in performance. Building strong muscles raises your metabolic rate, increases your endurance and you burn more calories all day long.

'Basically, the difference between fit people and unfit people is not in their hearts and lungs,' says cardiologist and fitness expert George Sheehan. 'What you train is muscle, to get more miles per gallon by increasing its ability to metabolise oxygen.'

In addition to the above benefits, strength training:

△   Builds stronger ligaments, tendons and muscles round a joint, giving protection to the joints.

△   Builds stronger limbs and torso for better lifting technique and protection for the lower back from injury.

△   Builds strong bones to reduce thinning and weakening of bones (osteoporosis).

△   Aids in improving posture.

The American College of Sports Medicine and other sports authorities now recommend two sessions of strength training per week in addition to a minimum of three sessions of aerobic training a week. To help you achieve the necessary strength training and to gain additional stretching and suppleness, we have provided The Whole Body Workout which, for maximum benefits, should be performed twice a week. You can perform this routine when you have finished your walkout and performed your post stretch, to give a complete all-over body-toning effect. Since your body is already warmed up, there is no need to do the warm-up exercises.

If you wish to follow the routine separately from your walk, at a time to suit your schedule, then make sure you begin with The Warm-up, followed by The Post Stretch (this includes The Quick Stretch), then The Whole Body Workout.

Similarly, perform The Whole Body Workout twice a week when exercising your options – mixing and matching walking with cycling or swimming. Either follow up your exercise session with The Post Stretch and The Whole Body Workout or perform The Warm-up, The Post Stretch and The Whole Body Workout at a time to suit yourself.

A low-impact aerobics class is different, in as much as the class will include a warm-up, stretch and body conditioning, so if you go to a LI aerobics class, you will perform at least the equivalent of one session of The Whole Body Workout. Then make sure that you do at least one more Whole Body Workout during the week.

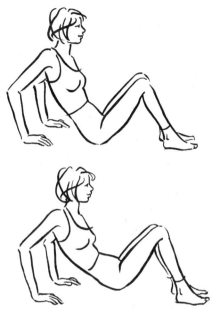

1 Tricep Dips

Sit on floor, legs bent, heels down. Bring arms behind, resting palms on floor, fingers forward. Slowly bend and extend arms. For a more advanced version, lift bottom off floor, using upper body weight for added resistance. Do 2 sets of 8.

2 Tricep Stretch

Sit on floor. Hold abdominals in and lengthen spine, legs in a comfortable position in front of you. Raise arms, bend right elbow, resting right hand on upper back. Hold just above right elbow with left hand. Slowly lift head up and ease it back against right arm until you feel a stretch in the back of the right arm. Hold 6 seconds. Repeat other side.

3 Press Ups
To strengthen arms and chest
On all fours, place hands directly under shoulders, fingers facing forward. Pull in abdominals and tilt pelvis to straighten back. Keep hips placed above your knees as you bend elbows lowering your forehead to the floor then push up straightening arms without locking into the elbow joints, or rounding shoulders. Keep the movement smooth with the head in line with the spine. Do 2–3 sets of 8.

4 Shoulder/Upper Arm Stretch
To ease upper arm and shoulders
From all fours, gently sit back over heels, keeping buttocks just above heels. Extend arms along the floor in front of you. Relax your head down and press palms into floor. Hold. Lengthen arms slightly more. Press palms again. Hold for 10–15 seconds.

5 Hip/Outer Thigh Lifts

To strengthen and tone hip and outer thigh

Lie on side with hips, shoulders and head in a straight line. Bend both knees to a 90 degree angle keeping them in line with your hips. Relax and let the upper body weight naturally fall forward. Hold abdominals in, back straight and top hip pressed forward. Lift and lower top leg, keeping knees in line, one above the other. Squeeze into outer thigh and hip as you lift. Repeat 10 times. Repeat on other leg.

6 Inner Thigh

To strengthen and tone inner thigh muscles

Lying on your side, as in Figure 5, from both knees bent, slowly extend out and straighten lower leg in line with the upper body. Keeping the upper leg bent and relaxed forward, slowly lift and lower bottom leg a few inches with the inside of your leg and foot facing the ceiling. Repeat 10 times. Repeat on other leg.

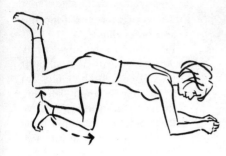

7 Buttock Squeeze
On elbows and knees, raise right leg until right leg is level with hip. Keeping the back straight and flat with tummy in, lower knee for 3 counts and raise knee for 1 count, squeezing buttock on the way up, relaxing it on the way down.

8 Cat Stretch
To stretch and maintain flexibility in lower back
Kneel with hands directly under shoulders and knees under hips. Relax head down and pull abdominals in round the back by pushing middle part of back towards ceiling. Now slowly and gently arch the back by pushing bottom up towards ceiling.

9 Pelvic Tilt
To strengthen abdominals
Lie on your back, hands by your sides, knees bent, feet flat on floor hip width apart. Pull in and flatten your tummy (abdominals) as you tilt the pelvis upwards and press lower back to the floor. There should be no 'space' between the lower back and floor as you adopt this position. Hold for 3 counts and release. Repeat 6 times.

10 Abdominal Curl

To strengthen and tone abdominals

Lie on your back, both knees bent, feet hip width apart and lower back pressed to the floor. With your hands behind your head, elbows out wide, ease head back into hands to support its weight. Now pull in and flatten tummy (abdominals) as you slowly lift head and shoulders 1 or 2 inches above the floor, then slowly lower. Keep head and neck in line with the spine. Chin up, head back and 'lift' leading with the chest. Exhale as you lift, inhale as you lower. Repeat 5–10 times.

11 Abdominal Oblique

To strengthen and tone waist

Lie on back as before, hands behind with elbows wide to support head. Pull in abdominals and press back into floor. Lift left shoulder with a slight rotation towards ceiling as the right hip and rib cage is squeezed together. Repeat 8 times and then workout other side of waist.

12 Knee Hug

To release tension in abdominals and ease out lower back

Lie on floor, knees bent. Slowly bring your knees into chest. Holding underneath the knee joints pull knees towards chest. The lower back and chest are relaxed to the floor. Hold for 10 seconds.

13 Abdominal Stretch

To stretch abdominals, rib cage, spine, shoulders, arms and feet

Lie on floor, knees bent. Slowly raise arms above head as you slide feet away to extend legs. Now point toes and fingers in opposite directions. To stop lower back from arching, slightly bend knees as you lengthen the whole body. Breathe deeply and gently increase the stretch as you exhale.

14 Spinal/Outer Thigh Stretch

To stretch lower back, outer thigh, hip and neck

Lie on back, both knees bent, feet on floor. Gently drop both legs to one side as you extend both arms from chest level and lower to other side. Look towards your hands to release your neck. Hold 5–10 seconds. Slowly lift knees and arms to centre. Repeat other side.

3

The Weight-off: The 30-Day Weight-loss Plan

The Pyramid Plan for eating is based on low-fat, high-fibre foods, and uses as its starting point The Healthy Eating Pyramid (see Figure 6). It emphasises the use of fresh foods, particularly fresh fruit and vegetables, and helps to reduce the consumption of fat and to increase the intake of complex carbohydrates (bread, potatoes, cereals, pasta and rice).

The recipes are not only balanced and nutritious, but also delicious, easy to prepare and versatile. The Pyramid Plan includes breakfasts, light meals and main meals, with suggestions for eating out and entertaining. It also offers a separate recipe section for maintaining The Pyramid Plan way of eating after the initial 30 days.

After following the 30-Day Plan, you will be able to adapt many of your own favourite recipes to a low-fat, high-fibre way of eating, using The Healthy Eating Pyramid as your guide (see also page 155, Identifying Fat and Fibre in Foods). If any foods in the recipes are not available, simply substitute another appropriate food. Eat plenty of fresh vegetables to complement the main course.

Choose whether you want the light meal or main meal at lunchtime or in the evening. If you are working, you may wish to take the light meal with you in a food container.

△ Radical Thinking: Food for Thought

Scientists now believe diet may play a prominent role in causing cancers. Cancers and heart disease are thought to

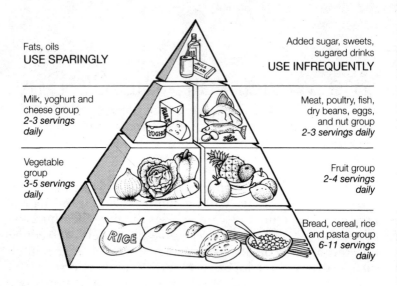

Fats, oils
USE SPARINGLY

Added sugar, sweets,
sugared drinks
USE INFREQUENTLY

Milk, yoghurt and
cheese group
*2-3 servings
daily*

Meat, poultry, fish,
dry beans, eggs,
and nut group
2-3 servings daily

Vegetable
group
*3-5 servings
daily*

Fruit group
*2-4 servings
daily*

Bread, cereal, rice
and pasta group
*6-11 servings
daily*

Figure 6

start with damage to cells caused by 'free radicals' – unstable molecules created by various normal chemical processes in the body or by environmental and other pollutants such as car fumes, radiation (including the sun's rays), alcohol and cigarette smoke. To protect our bodies from free radicals, antioxidants play a major part.

Antioxidants have the ability to transform and neutralise free radicals into less dangerous substances. A diet rich in antioxidant vitamins and minerals is now believed by scientists to be the best way of dealing with free radicals.

△ It's as Simple as A,C,E

'What is now called 'ACE' eating is all about eating enough foods rich in vitamins A (as beta-carotene), C and E. These essential vitamins are needed for a healthy immune system and to protect against cancer and heart disease. All three vitamins protect the body through their antioxidant powers. ACE vitamins are found in:

BETA-CAROTENE: dark green leafy vegetables, yellow and orange vegetables and fruits such as spinach, broccoli, peas, cress, asparagus, carrots, sweet potatoes, tomatoes, apricots, peaches, cherries, mangoes, cantaloup melon

VITAMIN C: citrus fruit, strawberries, blackcurrants, kiwi fruit, raw cabbage, green leafy vegetables, green peppers, potatoes, swedes, parsnips, tomatoes

VITAMIN E: nuts, seeds, whole grains, soya beans, vegetable oils (especially sunflower oil), fish liver oils, green leafy vegetables

Vitamin A in the form of beta-carotene, vitamin C and vitamin E mop up the destructive reactions caused by free radicals. Other free radical scavengers are the minerals selenium, zinc, manganese and copper. Selenium particularly has been singled out as an effective antioxidant and is available in such foods as liver, fish and shellfish, lamb, brown rice, muesli, milk and eggs, or is available in supplement form as Selenium ACE.

The World Health Organisation's recommendations that we should eat about 500 g (1 lb) of fresh fruit and vegetables a day is the best way to ensure that you get enough of the 'ACE' vitamins.

△ Fibre

Fibre is unrefined carbohydrate and is to be found in fruit and vegetables, bread, potatoes, nuts and pulses. Fibre, or roughage, passes through the digestive tract without being completely broken down and helps food and waste products to pass through the digestive system. It provides filling food without being fattening.

There are two types of fibre – soluble and insoluble. Soluble fibre is found in fruit, vegetables, oats and seeds. It is believed to help lower blood cholesterol levels and may decrease the likelihood of cardiovascular disease. As it may also slow down the entry of glucose into the bloodstream, it is particularly good for diabetics.

Insoluble fibre is to be found in whole grains and on the outside of fruit and seeds. The outer part, which is usually removed in the processing of foods, promotes more efficient elimination of waste from the body and may help in some digestive disorders, so it should be eaten. It helps prevent constipation, haemorrhoids, varicose veins and inflammation of the bowel.

The intake of fibre in the average Western diet has decreased at the same time that many physical disorders have increased. You should eat at least 30 g (1¼ oz) of fibre each day, but if you want to increase your fibre intake, you should do so gradually. It is best to eat fibre in complete foods, rather than adding bran to different dishes, for instance, as this way you eat it combined with other important nutrients. Fruit and vegetables are low-calorie sources of fibre, but they are also rich in vitamins and minerals. So eat more fruit and vegetables, with the skin on whenever possible, and eat less processed foods. Eat foods high in fibre at each meal and drink plenty of liquid.

△ Fish

Our bodies need fat. Fat is needed by the brain, muscles, heart, hair, skin, immune system and cell walls, etc. in order to function effectively. But in the average Western diet, too much fat is consumed – and of the wrong sort. Research studies show that among Greenland Eskimos, there is almost no record of heart disease, mainly because of the amount of seafood in their diet. Seafood contains Omega-3 fatty acids and it is these fatty acids which can play a significant role in preventing heart disease. High levels of these fish oils can be found in mackerel, herrings, salmon, sardines and tuna.

△ Salt

It is so easy to eat more salt than you actually need. Too much salt can contribute to high blood pressure which can increase the risk of heart disease. A lot of salt is found in processed foods – so check food labels. If you eat a balanced diet, you will get all the salt you need. To reduce your intake of salt, replace it over several weeks by using other flavourings, such as herbs and spices.

△ Breakfast

It is too easy to go off to work without first having breakfast. There are all sorts of excuses as to why breakfast was missed. But studies show that people who have breakfast are more alert in the morning than those who don't bother. Children who skip breakfast do not perform as well at school as their classmates who have breakfasted well.

Another problem is that if you don't have anything to eat beforework,youwillprobablystarttofeelhungrymid-morning. Chances are there won't be anything nourishing to eat, so you will settle for something that is less than adequate for a balanced diet.

When you are shopping, always make sure you have plenty of breakfast foods. Some people prefer to have more or less the same thing for breakfast each day, which is fine if it is nourishing – but why not try to vary your diet, even at breakfast-time. Maybe you have more time on a weekend, so you can have a more leisurely breakfast with plenty of variety.

Try and eat some carbohydrates, which are filling, but also have some fresh fruit and/or fruit juice. Here are some suggestions for Pyramid Plan breakfasts, from which you can choose your favourites – or work your way through them, one day after another. (Each is for one person.)

△   glass fresh orange juice
large slice wholemeal toast with 10 ml (2 tsp) marmalade or jam
apple

△ glass cranberry juice
large slice wholemeal toast with a poached egg

△ glass fresh orange juice
bowl of bran flakes with skimmed or semi-skimmed milk
peach

△ 1/2 grapefruit
large slice wholemeal toast with slices of grilled
tomato

△ glass apple juice
large slice wholemeal toast with baked beans

△ glass fresh orange juice
bowl of home-made muesli with skimmed or semi-
skimmed milk
pear

△ glass grapefruit juice
porridge made with skimmed or semi-skimmed milk
with 5 ml (1 tsp) honey

△ glass fresh orange juice
large slice wholemeal toast with grilled mushrooms

△ 1/2 pink grapefruit
slice lean cooked ham with large slice wholemeal
bread or toast

△ glass pink grapefruit juice
large slice wholemeal toast with scrambled egg made
in non-stick pan

When following The Pyramid Plan, eat fresh fruit after meals.
Fruit is often more appetising if cut up and presented in an
attractive way – apples, pears and oranges cut into segments,
pineapple cut into wedges, and plums and apricots halved
and dusted with cinnamon. After one meal in the day, eat
low-fat yogurt. There is a huge selection of fruit and natural
yogurts in the shops – or make your own.

△ Eating Out and Entertaining

Eating out is very much a part of many people's lives and you should not think that you cannot eat out if you are following The Pyramid Plan – the secret is to know which foods to choose. Most restaurants nowadays offer plenty of healthy, low-fat choices. Choose grilled fish or meat with vegetables served without added butter, or a salad as an accompaniment dressed with lemon juice or lime juice rather than an oily dressing. Avoid rich dishes with creamy sauces, and all fatty foods. For a dessert, choose fresh fruit – there is often quite a choice in restaurants.

If you are invited to a friend's house, obviously you cannot choose what you are going to eat. Just eat a moderate amount of whatever you are offered – and go for a longer walk than usual the next day!

When entertaining at home, prepare the main-meal recipe from The Pyramid Plan for that day or choose another main-meal recipe. Many of the light meals can be served as a first course when entertaining, such as Warm Salad with Prawns, or Antipasto. For dessert, there is nothing more attractive than a fresh fruit platter, with combinations of colours and tastes, using the now widely available exotic fruits along with more familiar fruits. Present the fruits on a large platter, garnished with sprigs of mint, for people to make their choice, and it will be a delicious ending to a nutritious and delicious meal. Or choose one of The Pyramid Plan desserts to be found on page 188.

You are now ready to begin Day 1 of your 30-Day Weight-loss Plan. You should begin this at the same time that you begin Day 1 of The 30-Day Walkout (see page 41). The following recipes are for two people, unless otherwise stated – halve quantities for one person or increase as necessary. So here goes. Start your Walkout and Weight-off now and begin burning away all those unwanted pounds.

DAY 1

▲ Light Meal

BROCCOLI AND SWEETCORN MAYONNAISE

125 g (5 oz) broccoli florets
1 corn on the cob, cooked
10 ml (2 tsp) reduced-calorie
  mayonnaise

10 ml (2 tsp) low-fat natural
  yogurt
cayenne pepper, to taste

Steam or boil the broccoli florets until tender then allow to cool. Cut the corn from the cob and mix with the mayonnaise and natural yogurt. Arrange the broccoli on individual plates and spoon over the corn mayonnaise. Sprinkle a little cayenne pepper on the salad. Serve with wholemeal bread.

▲ Main Meal

SPAGHETTI AL RAGU

150 g (6 oz) spaghetti
420g (15 oz) tin chopped
  tomatoes
220 g (8 oz) lean beef, ground
1 medium onion, chopped
100 g (4 oz) mushrooms,
  chopped

1 medium green pepper,
  chopped
5 ml (1 tsp) dried mixed
  herbs
freshly ground black pepper
Parmesan cheese, freshly
  grated (optional)

Cook the spaghetti as directed. Put the tomatoes, beef and onion into a large pan and cook over a medium heat for about 20 minutes, stirring occasionally. Add the mushrooms, green pepper, herbs and black pepper and cook for a further 5 minutes, adding some water if necessary. Put the spaghetti on to individual plates and spoon over the sauce. Serve with freshly grated Parmesan cheese if desired.

SPOTLIGHT   Complex carbohydrates are generally the least expensive foods but very nutritious. Jacket potatoes, pasta and salads are rich in carbohydrates but are not fattening, unless you cover them in calorie-laden dressings. Carbohydrates are usually more satisfying – they take up more room on your plate, and in your stomach, than fatty foods.

DAY 2

△ Light Meal

TUNA SALAD WITH BEANS

220g (8 oz) tin tuna in brine, drained
150 g (6 oz) cooked cannellini beans

juice of 1/2 lemon
1 shallot, finely chopped

Flake the tuna and gently mix with the cannellini beans and lemon juice. Spoon on to individual plates then add the finely chopped shallot. Serve with a crusty roll.

△ Main Meal

ROASTED VEGETABLE RATATOUILLE

1 large onion
1 large aubergine
2 large courgettes
1 red pepper
1 green pepper
4 medium tomatoes

2 cloves garlic
5 ml (1 tsp) tomato purée
3 ml (1/2 tsp) dried mixed herbs
freshly ground black pepper and salt

Heat the oven to Gas Mark 6 (200°C/400°F). Put all the vegetables, whole, in an ovenproof dish and roast for 30–40 minutes, turning occasionally. Remove the skin from the onion, aubergine, peppers and garlic then chop the flesh of all the vegetables. Put into a pan with the tomato purée, herbs, black pepper and salt, adding a little water. Combine all ingredients thoroughly and heat through. Serve with wedges of fresh wholemeal bread.

SPOTLIGHT   Following a very low-calorie diet, you would probably be losing out on essential vitamins and minerals. When following The Pyramid Plan, you eat a healthy, balanced diet, full of nutritious and delicious foods.

DAY 3

△ Light Meal

EGG AND WATERCRESS PITTA SANDWICH WITH CRUDITÉS

2 pitta breads
5 ml (1 tsp) reduced-calorie
  mayonnaise
bunch of watercress

2 hard-boiled eggs
batons of carrot, celery,
  green and red peppers, of
  your choice

Open the pitta bread and spread the mayonnaise inside. Put a layer of watercress into the bread. Slice the eggs then arrange on the watercress. Serve with your choice of crudités.

△ Main Meal

GRILLED FISH WITH POTATO AND SALAD

2 × 150 g (6 oz) fillets of white
  fish, such as cod, haddock
  or coley

5 ml (1 tsp) olive oil
freshly ground black pepper
2 lemon wedges

Brush the fish fillets with olive oil and add some freshly ground black pepper. Cook under a preheated grill for about 15 minutes, turning occasionally to cook evenly. Put on to individual plates and garnish with a wedge of lemon. Serve with jacket or new potatoes and a mixed salad.

SPOTLIGHT   It's a good idea to eat something light before exercising if you haven't eaten for some time, particularly first thing in the morning. Fruit is a good choice – and bananas are particularly popular as an energy booster.

DAY 4

△ Light Meal

COTTAGE CHEESE, TOMATO AND KIWI FRUIT SALAD

150 g (6 oz) low-fat cottage
  cheese

2 tomatoes
2 kiwi fruit

Spoon the cottage cheese on to individual plates. Slice the tomatoes and peel and slice the kiwi fruit. Arrange alternate slices of tomato and kiwi fruit on the cottage cheese. Serve with wholemeal bread.

△ Main Meal

SWEET AND SOUR VEGETABLES

100 g (4 oz) mangetout
100 g (4 oz) baby sweetcorn
1 medium red pepper, sliced
100 g (4 oz) button
  mushrooms
10 ml (2 tsp) white wine
  vinegar

10 ml (2 tsp) soy sauce
10 ml (2 tsp) clear honey
juice of 1 orange
freshly ground black pepper
  and salt
100 g (4 oz) bean sprouts
4 spring onions, sliced

Simmer the mangetout, sweetcorn, red pepper and mushrooms in a little water for 5 minutes. If the water has not evaporated, drain. Mix together the wine vinegar, soy sauce, honey, orange juice, black pepper and salt and stir into the vegetable mixture over a low heat. Add the bean sprouts and spring onions and heat through. Serve with brown rice.

SPOTLIGHT   When you exercise aerobically you not only increase your metabolism at the time you are exercising but for some time afterwards – and an increased metabolism is good news when you are trying to lose weight.

DAY 5

△ Light Meal

PRAWN MAYONNAISE SANDWICH

150 g (6 oz) cooked peeled
  prawns
10 ml (2 tsp) reduced-calorie
  mayonnaise

5 ml (1 tsp) lemon juice
4 slices granary bread

Mix together the mayonnaise and lemon juice then coat the
prawns with this mixture. Make up two sandwiches with the
slices of granary bread. Cut into quarters and serve garnished
with wedges of tomato.

△ Main Meal

CHICKEN KORMA

2 chicken breast fillets, skin
  removed, cut into small
  pieces
10 ml (2 tsp) sunflower oil
1 medium onion, chopped
10 ml (2 tsp) ground
  coriander
5 ml (1 tsp) ground cumin

5 ml (1 tsp) ground turmeric
100 g (4 oz) mushrooms,
  chopped
freshly ground black pepper
125 g (5 oz) low-fat natural
  yogurt
25 g (1 oz) flaked almonds,
  toasted

Heat the sunflower oil in a large pan then add the onion,
chicken and ground spices and cook over a medium heat
for about 15 minutes, stirring to prevent sticking. Add the
mushrooms and black pepper and cook for a further 5
minutes, stirring occasionally. At the last moment, stir in
the natural yogurt. Serve with basmati rice on individual
plates and garnish with toasted almonds.

SPOTLIGHT   For a busy person, a short time spent on 'you' at the end of the day is a real treat. When you've worked hard, exercised and eaten healthily, take 15–30 minutes to relax. It might be listening to music, having a bath or giving yourself a manicure. Whatever your choice, relax and enjoy yourself.

DAY 6

△ Light Meal

WARM SALAD WITH MUSHROOMS

150 g (6 oz) mushrooms, chopped
5 ml (1 tsp) olive oil
5 ml (1 tsp) balsamic vinegar
10 ml (2 tsp) lemon juice
2 spring onions, shredded
5 ml (1 tsp) chopped fresh parsley
lettuce leaves
freshly ground black pepper
2 lemon wedges

Heat the olive oil gently in a small pan and sauté the mushrooms for 3 or 4 minutes. Add the balsamic vinegar and lemon juice then stir in the spring onions and parsley. Arrange the lettuce leaves on individual plates then spoon over the mushrooms and warm vinaigrette. Add some freshly ground black pepper and garnish with a wedge of lemon. Serve with wholemeal bread.

△ Main Meal

PASTA MARINARA

150 g (6 oz) pasta
1 medium onion, chopped
1 clove garlic, finely chopped
2 medium tomatoes, chopped
1 glass white wine
4 baby squid, cleaned and cut into rings
1 small green pepper, diced
100 g (4 oz) mushrooms, chopped
chilli sauce, to taste
5 ml (1 tsp) dried mixed herbs
freshly ground black pepper
150 g (6 oz) cooked peeled prawns

Cook the pasta as directed. Put the onion, garlic, tomatoes and white wine into a pan and cook over a medium heat for 5 minutes, stirring occasionally. Add the squid, green pepper, mushrooms, chilli sauce, herbs and black pepper and cook for a further 5 minutes, adding more wine if necessary. Finally, add the prawns and heat thoroughly. Serve the pasta on individual plates with the marinara sauce poured over.

SPOTLIGHT   Pamper your feet! They are looking after you while you exercise – so look after them. Soak your feet in water for 10–15 minutes, dry them thoroughly then feed them with your favourite moisturising cream.

DAY 7

⚠ Light Meal

JACKET POTATO WITH CHICORY AND ORANGE SALAD

2 large baking potatoes
1 large orange, peeled and cut into segments
1 head chicory, sliced

10 ml (2 tsp) low-fat natural yogurt
paprika, to taste

Bake the potatoes. Reserve 4 orange segments then chop the remaining segments and mix with the slices of chicory and the natural yogurt. Cut the potatoes in half lengthways and put on individual plates with the cut side up. Spoon the salad on to the potato and garnish with the reserved orange segments. Sprinkle a little paprika on the salad.

⚠ Main Meal

PORK WITH FENNEL

220 g (8 oz) pork fillet, cut into bite-size pieces
1 medium onion, chopped
1 fennel bulb, trimmed, cored and cut into quarters
300 ml (10 fl oz) tomato passata

10 ml (2 tsp) white wine vinegar
5 ml (1 tsp) dried mixed herbs
100 g (4 oz) mushrooms, sliced
freshly ground black pepper and salt

Put the pork fillet, onion and fennel into a large pan and add the tomato passata, white wine vinegar and herbs. Bring to the boil then simmer over a medium heat for about 25 minutes or until the meat is tender. Stir occasionally, adding some water if necessary. Add the mushrooms, some freshly ground black pepper and salt and cook for a further 5 minutes. Serve with brown rice and broccoli or spinach.

SPOTLIGHT   Be patient. Regular aerobic exercise combined with a healthy diet really does work. Not only will you be healthier, slimmer and more toned-up, but you will feel less stressed and have more energy and enthusiasm.

DAY 8

⚠ Light Meal

SMOKED MACKEREL SALAD

1 smoked mackerel fillet	juice of 1/2 lemon
wedge of cucumber, diced	lettuce leaves
1 apple, cored and sliced	

Flake the mackerel and mix with the diced cucumber, slices of apple and lemon juice. Arrange the lettuce leaves on individual plates and spoon the mackerel salad on to the lettuce leaves.

⚠ Main Meal

ROASTED AUBERGINE AND PEPPERS

1 large aubergine	10 ml (2 tsp) balsamic
1 large red pepper	vinegar
1 large green pepper	fresh basil leaves
	freshly ground black pepper

Heat the oven to Gas Mark 6 (200°C/400°F). Put the aubergine and peppers into a heatproof dish and bake for 30–40 minutes, turning occasionally. The skins of the peppers will probably become charred, but they can easily be removed when cooked. Cut the ends from the aubergine then cut in half lengthways. Cut the peppers into sections and arrange with the aubergine on serving dishes. Drizzle the balsamic vinegar over the vegetables and add basil leaves and black pepper to taste. Serve with wedges of fresh wholemeal bread.

SPOTLIGHT Don't try to skip meals, in the hope of losing weight more quickly. Make sure you eat regularly. If you skip meals, you'll get hungry and will be more likely to give in to temptation.

DAY 9

▲ Light Meal

TOMATO SALAD PITTA SANDWICH
WITH CRUDITÉS

2 large tomatoes
2 spring onions
10 ml (2 tsp) reduced-calorie
  mayonnaise
10 ml (2 tsp) low-fat natural
  yogurt

cayenne pepper, to taste
2 pitta breads
batons of carrot, celery,
  green and red peppers, of
  your choice

Chop the tomatoes and spring onions into small pieces then
mix with the mayonnaise, yogurt and cayenne pepper. Open
the pitta bread and spoon in the tomato salad. Serve with
your choice of crudités.

▲ Main Meal

CHILLI CON CARNE

300 g (10 oz) minced turkey
  or ground beef
1 medium onion, chopped
420 g (15 oz) tin chopped
  tomatoes
chilli powder or sauce, to
  taste
1 medium green pepper,
  chopped

100 g (4 oz) mushrooms,
  chopped
10 ml (2 tsp) tomato purée
5 ml (1 tsp) dried mixed
  herbs
freshly ground black pepper
420 g (15 oz) tin cooked
  red kidney beans, drained
  (if using dried, cook as
  directed)

Put the meat, onion, chopped tomatoes and chilli powder
or sauce into a large pan and cook over a medium heat
for about 20 minutes, stirring occasionally. Add the green
pepper, mushrooms, tomato purée and herbs and cook

for a further 5 minutes. Add some black pepper and adjust the chilli seasoning to taste then stir in the cooked red kidney beans and heat through. Serve with brown rice.

SPOTLIGHT   When choosing a snack, just think: a medium pear contains 0.7 g of fat, 4.5 g of dietary fibre and 80 calories, the sugar being fructose (fruit sugar), whereas a 50 g (2 oz) chocolate bar contains 25 g of fat (mainly saturated), 17 g of refined sugar, 0.1 g of dietary fibre and 300 calories. And the pear will raise and maintain your blood sugar levels and energy for much longer than the chocolate bar.

DAY 10

△ Light Meal

GREEK SALAD

lettuce leaves
2 tomatoes
1 small green pepper
wedge of cucumber

50 g (2 oz) feta cheese
8 black olives
juice of 1/2 lemon

Arrange the lettuce leaves on individual plates. Slice the tomato, green pepper and cucumber then arrange on the lettuce leaves. Cut the feta cheese into small cubes and add to the salad with the olives and lemon juice. Serve with wholemeal pitta bread.

△ Main Meal

MUSHROOM STROGANOFF

440 g (1 lb) mushrooms, chopped (use a mixture of oyster, chestnut, shiitake and cup, if possible)
5 ml (1 tsp) sunflower oil
1 medium onion, chopped
1 clove garlic, finely chopped
100 g (4 oz) low-fat natural yogurt or fromage frais

5 ml (1 tsp) tomato purée
3 ml (1/2 tsp) paprika
3 ml (1/2 tsp) dried mixed herbs
freshly ground black pepper and salt

Heat the oil gently in a large pan and cook the onion and garlic for 5 minutes. Add the mushrooms and cook for a further 5 minutes. Mix together the tomato purée, paprika, herbs, black pepper and salt with a few drops of water and add to the mushrooms, combining all ingredients thoroughly. Stir in the natural yogurt or fromage frais, and heat through. Serve with basmati rice.

SPOTLIGHT   Drink lots of water every day. It helps to fill your body's needs, providing an important calorie-free nutrient. And it keeps your skin, nails and hair in good condition and prevents any feeling of dehydration.

DAY 11

△ Light Meal

GARDEN SALAD

2 medium carrots, grated
1 stick celery, thinly sliced
2 medium tomatoes, sliced
wedge of cucumber, sliced

1 large pear, cored and cut
   into small pieces
juice of 1/2 lemon
freshly ground black pepper
2 sprigs fresh mint

Put the grated carrot on individual plates then add the celery.
Arrange alternate slices of tomato and cucumber on the salad
then add the pieces of pear. Add the lemon juice and some
freshly ground black pepper. Garnish with a sprig of mint.

△ Main Meal

TUNA AND BEAN RAGOÛT

220 g (8 oz) tin tuna in brine,
   drained and flaked
420 g (15 oz) tin cooked
   red kidney beans, drained
   (if using dried, cook as
   directed)
1 large onion, chopped
4 medium tomatoes, chopped

5 ml (1 tsp) dried mixed
   herbs
1 medium green pepper,
   chopped
10 ml (2 tsp) Nam Pla fish
   sauce
freshly ground black pepper

Put the chopped onion, tomatoes and herbs into a pan with
125 ml (5 fl oz) water and cook over a medium heat for 5
minutes, then add the green pepper and cook for a further 5
minutes, stirring occasionally to prevent sticking. Reduce the
liquid if necessary. Stir in the fish sauce then add the tuna, red
kidney beans and some freshly ground black pepper. Heat
thoroughly then serve with jacket potatoes and broccoli or
spinach.

SPOTLIGHT   One way to eat less calories without having to try too hard is to use more vegetables and less meat in your favourite recipes. Or serve yourself a smaller portion of your meal and garnish it with a side salad.

DAY 12

△ Light Meal

BEEF SANDWICH

125 g (5 oz) lean cooked
  beef, thinly sliced
mustard

4 slices granary bread
gherkins

Spread some mustard on two slices of bread. Arrange the slices of beef on the bread and make up two sandwiches. Cut into quarters and serve garnished with gherkins.

△ Main Meal

SPAGHETTI ALLA PUTTANESCA

150 g (6 oz) spaghetti
420 g (15 oz) tin chopped
  tomatoes
1 medium onion, chopped
1 clove garlic, finely chopped
2 anchovy fillets, chopped

10 ml (2 tsp) capers
5 ml (1 tsp) dried mixed
  herbs
freshly ground black pepper
8 black olives, pitted

Cook the spaghetti as directed. Put the tomatoes, onion and garlic into a pan and cook over a medium heat for 5 minutes. Add the anchovies, capers and herbs and cook for a further 5 minutes, reducing the liquid if necessary. Put the spaghetti on to individual plates and spoon over the sauce, adding the black pepper and olives as a garnish.

SPOTLIGHT Be adventurous when buying fresh fruit and vegetables. There is so much choice of foods from all over the world nowadays, and most supermarkets are very helpful in explaining how to prepare these foods. If you don't know what to do with a certain food – ask!

DAY 13

⚠ Light Meal

COURGETTE FRITTATA

2 medium courgettes, sliced
3 large eggs
freshly ground black pepper
  and salt
3 ml (1/2 tsp) dried mixed
  herbs

5 ml (1 tsp) olive oil
50 g (2 oz) low-fat cheese,
  grated
2 sprigs fresh parsley

Grill the slices of courgette for about 5 minutes, turning to cook evenly.

Meanwhile, whisk the eggs with a little water, some freshly ground black pepper and salt. Add the herbs. Heat the olive oil in a small omelette pan and add the eggs, cooking until almost set. Add the grated cheese then finish cooking under a hot grill. Arrange the courgettes on the omelette, fold over and cut in half. Serve on individual plates, garnished with a sprig of parsley.

⚠ Main Meal

CHICKEN WITH COUSCOUS

2 chicken breast fillets, skin
  removed, cut into small
  pieces
1 red onion, chopped
10 ml (2 tsp) ground
  coriander
5 ml (1 tsp) ground cumin
5 ml (1 tsp) ground cinnamon
3 ml (1/2 tsp) grated lemon
  zest

juice of 1 lemon
10 ml (2 tsp) tomato purée
freshly ground black pepper
  and salt
1 small green pepper,
  chopped
1 small red pepper, chopped
25 g (1 oz) sultanas
75 g (3 oz) couscous,
  prepared as indicated on
  the packet

Put the chicken and onion into a pan, cover with water and cook over a medium heat for 15 minutes, stirring occasionally. Reduce the liquid to about 15 ml (1 tbsp). Mix together the coriander, cumin, cinnamon, lemon zest and juice, tomato purée, black pepper and salt and pour over the chicken. Add the green and red peppers and sultanas, stir thoroughly and cook for a further 5 minutes. Serve on a bed of couscous, with broccoli.

SPOTLIGHT   On Saturdays or Sundays (both if possible) do something different from your normal routine. Whether you visit an art gallery, buy a new book or visit someone you know is lonely, if it seems worthwhile to you, then it is worth doing.

DAY 14

△ Light Meal

FRENCH BREAD PIZZA

2 × 13 cm (5 inch) wedges of French bread, cut length-ways
1 small onion, finely chopped
1 clove garlic, finely chopped
2 medium tomatoes, chopped
3 ml (1/2 tsp) dried mixed herbs
8 thin slices salami
8 black olives
100g (4 oz) Italian Mozzarella cheese, grated

Put the onion, garlic, tomatoes and herbs into a small pan with 15 ml (1 tbsp) water and cook over a medium heat for 8 minutes, stirring occasionally. Reduce the liquid if necessary. Toast the bread on both sides. Spread the tomato mixture on to the toast then add the salami and olives and finally the cheese. Grill until golden.

△ Main Meal

PRAWNS AND AVOCADO WITH RICE

150 g (6 oz) long-grain rice
150 g (6 oz) cooked peeled prawns
10 ml (2 tsp) olive oil
1 small onion, finely chopped
50 g (2 oz) mushrooms, thinly sliced
10 ml (2 tsp) chopped fresh dill
10 ml (2 tsp) Nam Pla fish sauce
1 small avocado
freshly ground black pepper

Cook the rice as directed, drain and keep warm. Meanwhile, heat the olive oil in a pan and cook the onion over a medium heat for 5 minutes then add the mushrooms and cook for a further 5 minutes, stirring to prevent sticking. Add the dill and fish sauce to the onion and mushrooms then add the prawns and heat through thoroughly. Stir the rice into the prawn mixture, adding a little water if necessary. Peel and dice the avocado and gently fold into the prawns and rice. Add some freshly ground black pepper. Serve with sweetcorn.

SPOTLIGHT Remember that to keep your new habits up, life should be fun. Vary your exercise and vary your diet. There's so much choice with The Pyramid Plan, so exercise your options to the full. And give yourself plenty of treats – not all treats have to be laden with calories!

DAY 15

△ Light Meal

COTTAGE CHEESE, CUCUMBER AND PEACH SALAD

150 g (6 oz) low-fat cottage cheese

wedge of cucumber
2 peaches

Spoon the cottage cheese on to individual plates. Slice the cucumber and peaches. Arrange alternate slices of cucumber and peaches on the cottage cheese. Serve with wholemeal bread.

△ Main Meal

SOYA BEAN RAGOÛT

420 g (15 oz) tin cooked soya beans, drained (if using dried, cook as directed)
1 medium onion, chopped
1 clove garlic, finely chopped
1 large carrot, sliced
1 stick celery, sliced

4 medium tomatoes, chopped
1 medium red pepper, chopped
100 g (4 oz) mushrooms, chopped
chilli sauce, to taste
freshly ground black pepper

Put the onion, garlic, carrot, celery and tomatoes into a pan with 125 ml (5 fl oz) water and cook over a medium heat for 10 minutes, stirring occasionally to prevent sticking. Add the red pepper and mushrooms and cook for a further 5 minutes. Reduce the liquid if necessary. Add the cooked soya beans, chilli sauce to taste and some freshly ground black pepper, and heat thoroughly. Serve with jacket potatoes and cauliflower.

SPOTLIGHT   When dieting without exercising, about one-third of the weight lost is from lean tissue, not fat tissue, leading to weakness and muscle wasting. Good reason to keep exercising?!

DAY 16

△ Light Meal

EGG SALAD PITTA SANDWICH WITH CRUDITÉS

2 pitta breads
5 ml (1 tsp) reduced-calorie
  mayonnaise
lettuce leaves
2 hard-boiled eggs

wedge of cucumber
batons of carrot, celery,
  green and red peppers, of
  your choice

Open the pitta bread and spread the mayonnaise inside. Shred the lettuce leaves and put a layer on the bread. Slice the eggs and cucumber and arrange on the lettuce. Serve with your choice of crudités.

△ Main Meal

PORK MEAT BALLS

220 g (8 oz) lean pork,
  minced
1 small onion, grated
5 ml (1 tsp) garam masala or
  curry powder
5 ml (1 tsp) lemon juice

freshly ground black pepper
  and salt
cornflour
lettuce leaves, shredded
2 lemon wedges

Mix together the pork, onion, garam masala or curry powder, lemon juice, black pepper and salt then separate into 8 balls. Roll in cornflour then grill under a preheated grill for about 15 minutes, turning to cook evenly. Arrange on individual plates, garnished with shredded lettuce and lemon wedges. Serve with brown rice and broad beans.

> *SPOTLIGHT* The more oxygen you process, the more body fat you burn up. So activities that increase your consumption of oxygen also increase the burning of fat. And what's more, oxygen is free!

DAY 17

◭ Light Meal

TUNA, APPLE AND TOASTED PINE NUT SALAD

220 g (8 oz) tin tuna in brine, drained
1 apple, cut into small pieces
10 ml (2 tsp) reduced-calorie mayonnaise
5 ml (1 tsp) lemon juice

5 ml (1 tsp) chopped fresh dill
radicchio or other salad leaf
freshly ground black pepper
50 g (2 oz) pine nuts, lightly toasted

Gently mix the tuna and apple with the mayonnaise, lemon juice and dill. Put the radicchio or other salad leaves on individual plates and spoon the salad on to the leaves. Add some freshly ground black pepper and garnish with the lightly toasted pine nuts.

◭ Main Meal

INDIAN VEGETABLES

1 medium onion, chopped
1 large aubergine, cubed
220g (8 oz) tin tomatoes
1 medium green pepper, chopped
100 g (4 oz) mushrooms, chopped

10 ml (2 tsp) ground coriander
5 ml (1 tsp) ground cumin
chilli sauce, to taste
freshly ground black pepper
100 g (4 oz) cooked red kidney beans

Put the onion, aubergine and tomatoes into a large pan and cook over a medium heat for 8 minutes. Add the green pepper, mushrooms and all seasonings and cook for a further 5 minutes. Add the kidney beans to warm through. Serve with basmati rice.

SPOTLIGHT   Have you ever wished that it was lettuce leaves that were full of calories and chocolate that could be eaten ad infinitum?! If you are trying to wean yourself from fattening foods, take one problem at a time. Work, for example, on attacking the sweet tooth first, and then getting away from savoury snacks.

DAY 18

▲ Light Meal

TOMATO AND LENTIL SALAD

220 g (8oz) cooked lentils
5 ml (1 tsp) reduced-calorie
  mayonnaise
10 ml (2 tsp) low-fat natural
  yogurt

5 ml (1 tsp) chopped fresh
  mint
2 tomatoes
freshly ground black pepper

Mix together the mayonnaise, natural yogurt and mint then coat the lentils with this mixture. Spoon on to individual plates. Slice the tomatoes, arrange on the lentils, and season with black pepper. Serve with wholemeal bread.

▲ Main Meal

MUSHROOM AND FISH PASTA

150 g (6 oz) pasta
1 medium onion, chopped
100 g (4 oz) petits pois
150 g (6 oz) mushrooms,
  chopped (use a variety of
  types if possible)
220 g (8 oz) skinless fillets
  of white fish, cut into bite-
  size pieces

125 ml (5 fl oz) low-fat single
  cream
10 ml (2 tsp) Nam Pla fish
  sauce
10 ml (2 tsp) chopped fresh
  dill

Cook the pasta as directed. Put the onion and petits pois in a pan with 125 ml (5 fl oz) water and cook over a medium heat for 5 minutes. Add the mushrooms and pieces of fish and cook for a further 8 minutes, stirring occasionally to prevent sticking. Reduce the liquid if necessary. Stir in the cream, fish sauce and dill. Serve the pasta on individual plates and spoon the mushroom and fish sauce on to the pasta.

SPOTLIGHT   Read labels on foods when shopping. Food manufacturers are getting used to the idea that people want to eat more healthily so they are having to become more health-conscious. There are also more reduced-fat versions of foods available.

DAY 19

△ Light Meal

HAM AND CHEESE SANDWICH WITH CRUDITÉS

2 slices lean cooked ham
75 g (3 oz) low-fat cheese, grated
4 slices granary bread

mustard
batons of carrot, celery, green and red peppers, of your choice

Arrange the slices of ham and the grated cheese on two slices of granary bread. Spread some mustard on the other slices then make up the sandwiches. Cut into quarters and serve with your choice of crudités.

△ Main Meal

VEGETABLE KEBABS

1 large aubergine
1 large courgette
1 medium onion
1 large red pepper
1 large green pepper

lemon juice
dash of chilli sauce
freshly ground black pepper and salt

Cut the vegetables into large pieces. Mix together the lemon juice, chilli sauce, black pepper and salt and pour over the vegetables. Leave for 30 minutes, if possible. Arrange the vegetables on four skewers and grill for 10 minutes, turning as necessary. Serve on a bed of rice.

SPOTLIGHT   Keep your fridge and cupboards well stocked with healthy, appetising foods – fresh fruit, vegetables, pasta and rice are the basis of delicious and nourishing meals.

DAY 20

△ Light Meal

JACKET POTATO WITH CHILLI BEANS

2 large baking potatoes	10 ml (2 tsp) tomato purée
220 g (8 oz) cooked red	10 ml (2 tsp) lemon juice
kidney beans	chilli sauce, to taste

Bake the potatoes. Heat the red kidney beans with the mixture of tomato purée, lemon juice and chilli sauce to taste. Cut the potatoes in half lengthways and put on individual plates with the cut side up. Spoon the chilli beans over the potatoes.

△ Main Meal

FISH CASSEROLE

220 g (8 oz) skinless fillets of white fish	100 g (4 oz) mushrooms, chopped
420g (15 oz) tin chopped tomatoes	5 ml (1 tsp) dried mixed herbs
1 medium onion, chopped	10 ml (2 tsp) Nam Pla fish sauce
100 g (4 oz) petits pois	
1 small green pepper, chopped	freshly ground black pepper

Put the chopped tomatoes, onion, petits pois and fish fillets into a large pan and cook over a medium heat for about 8 minutes. Stir in the green pepper, mushrooms and dried mixed herbs and simmer for a further 5 minutes. Add the fish sauce, some freshly ground black pepper and a little water if necessary. Stir gently, breaking the fish into bite-size pieces. Serve with cauliflower and wedges of fresh wholemeal bread.

> *SPOTLIGHT*   Avoid eating between meals. But if you really feel hungry, have fresh fruit or raw vegetables as a snack – they are healthy, nutritious fast foods!

DAY 21

△ Light Meal

WARM SALAD WITH ROAST PEPPERS

1 medium red pepper
1 medium green pepper
5 ml (1 tsp) olive oil
1 shallot, finely chopped

5 ml (1 tsp) white wine
  vinegar
5 ml (1 tsp) lemon juice
lettuce leaves
freshly ground black pepper

Roast the whole red and green peppers in a preheated oven, Gas Mark 6 (200°C/400°F) for 30 minutes, turning once or twice. Put the roasted peppers into a plastic food bag and after a few minutes the skin may be easily removed. Reserve the juice and keep the peppers warm. Heat the olive oil gently in a small pan and add the chopped shallot. Cook for 5 minutes, stirring to prevent sticking. Add the white wine vinegar and lemon juice and heat through then add the juice from the peppers. Arrange the lettuce leaves on individual plates. Cut each pepper into four pieces and arrange on the lettuce. Spoon the shallot and warm vinaigrette over the salad and add some freshly ground black pepper. Serve with wholemeal bread.

△ Main Meal

LAMB WITH CHICK PEAS AND MINT

220 g (8 oz) lean lamb,
  minced
1 medium onion, chopped
300 ml (10 fl oz) tomato
  passata
100 g (4 oz) mushrooms,
  thinly sliced

10 ml (2 tsp) chopped fresh
  mint
juice of 1/2 lemon
freshly ground black pepper
420g (15 oz) tin cooked chick
  peas, drained (if using
  dried, cook as directed)

Put the lamb, onion and tomato passata into a pan and cook over a medium heat for 20 minutes, stirring occasionally. Add the mushrooms, mint, lemon juice, and freshly ground black pepper and cook for a further 5 minutes. Finally, add the cooked chick peas and heat thoroughly. Serve with rice or couscous.

SPOTLIGHT   Only 10 days to go with your Weight-off plan – and you should be thoroughly enjoying it! Don't forget to keep planning what meals you're going to have in advance. It's nice to look forward to them.

DAY 22

△ Light Meal

CHEESE AND TOMATO SANDWICH
WITH CRUDITÉS

2 tomatoes
75 g (3 oz) low-fat cheese,
   grated
4 slices granary bread

batons of carrot, celery,
   green and red peppers, of
   your choice

Slice the tomatoes and arrange on two slices of bread. Add
the grated cheese and make up two sandwiches. Cut into
quarters and serve with your choice of crudités.

△ Main Meal

POACHED SALMON AND SALAD

2 × 125 g (5 oz) fillets of fresh
   salmon
300 ml (10 fl oz) vegetable
   stock

5 ml (1 tsp) dried mixed
   herbs
freshly ground black pepper

Poach the salmon for about 8 minutes in the vegetable stock
with the herbs and some freshly ground black pepper. Serve
on individual plates with a mixed salad and jacket or new
potatoes.

> *SPOTLIGHT*   Not all the food you eat needs to be exercised
> off! Your body needs calories just to maintain its normal
> functions. It's all the extras you need to be aware of – the
> cakes, biscuits, ice-cream and chocolates – that can help the
> pounds creep on. Just don't let them.

DAY 23

△ Light Meal

CHICKEN, KIWI FRUIT AND TOMATO SALAD

1 cooked chicken breast
   fillet, skin removed
5 ml (1 tsp) reduced-calorie
   mayonnaise
10 ml (2 tsp) low-fat natural
   yogurt
lettuce leaves
2 tomatoes
2 kiwi fruit

Mix together the mayonnaise and yogurt. Break the chicken fillet into small pieces and coat with the mayonnaise and yogurt. Put the lettuce leaves on to individual plates and spoon the chicken on to the lettuce. Slice the tomatoes, and peel and slice the kiwi fruit, then arrange alternate slices around the chicken. Serve with wholemeal bread.

△ Main Meal

BEAN GOULASH WITH RED CABBAGE

125 g (5 oz) cooked red
   kidney beans
125 g (5 oz) cooked white
   haricot beans
420 g (15 oz) tin chopped
   tomatoes
1 medium onion, chopped
wedge of red cabbage,
   chopped
100 g (4 oz) mushrooms,
   chopped
1 medium red pepper,
   chopped
10 ml (2 tsp) tomato purée
5 ml (1 tsp) dried mixed
   herbs
10 ml (2 tsp) paprika
freshly ground black pepper
   and salt
15 ml (1 tbsp) low-fat natural
   yogurt

Put the chopped tomatoes, onion and red cabbage into a large pan and cook over a medium heat for 5 minutes. Add the mushrooms and red pepper and simmer for a further 5 minutes. Stir in the tomato purée, dried mixed herbs, paprika, black pepper and salt, adding a little water if necessary. Add the red kidney beans and white haricot beans and heat through. At the last moment stir in the natural yogurt. Serve with jacket or new potatoes.

> *SPOTLIGHT*   Don't be afraid to try new foods and recipes – variety is very important and it is for taste that we eat, as well as for hunger.

DAY 24

△ Light Meal

EGG AND WATERCRESS SALAD

bunch of watercress
wedge of cucumber, sliced
2 hard-boiled eggs, quartered

10 ml (2 tsp) lemon juice
5 ml (1 tsp) balsamic vinegar

Arrange the watercress and cucumber slices on individual plates. Add the quarters of hard-boiled egg. Mix together the lemon juice and balsamic vinegar and spoon on to the salad. Serve with a bread roll.

△ Main Meal

TURKEY VESUVIUS

2 × 125 g (5 oz) turkey breast
   fillets
2 medium tomatoes, sliced
4 slices Italian Mozzarella
   cheese

freshly ground black pepper
2 lemon wedges
fresh basil leaves

Grill the turkey breast fillets under a medium heat for about 20 minutes or until golden, turning occasionally. Arrange the slices of tomato on the turkey fillets and the Mozzarella cheese on the tomato. Return to the grill for 2 minutes. Add some freshly ground black pepper, a wedge of lemon and some basil leaves. Serve with green beans and wedges of fresh wholemeal bread.

SPOTLIGHT Be creative and versatile when cooking. If you haven't got an ingredient for a recipe, think what you could use as a substitute. It's more fun if the same dish is never cooked the same way twice!

DAY 25

△ Light Meal

SALMON SANDWICH WITH CRUDITÉS

125 g (5 oz) tinned salmon
5 ml (1 tsp) reduced-calorie
  mayonnaise
4 slices granary bread

batons of carrot, celery,
  green and red peppers, of
  your choice

Mix together the salmon and mayonnaise. Make up two sandwiches with the granary bread. Cut into quarters and serve with your choice of crudités.

△ Main Meal

PASTA WITH ROASTED VEGETABLES

1 medium onion
1 medium aubergine
1 small green pepper
1 small red pepper
150 g (6 oz) pasta
300 ml (10 fl oz) tomato
  passata
100 g (4 oz) mushrooms,
  chopped

5 ml (1 tsp) dried mixed
  herbs
chilli sauce, to taste
freshly ground black pepper
1/2 Italian Mozzarella
  cheese, cut into small
  pieces

Heat the oven to Gas Mark 6 (200°C/400°F). Put the onion, aubergine and green and red peppers into an ovenproof dish and bake for 30–40 minutes, turning occasionally. Remove the skin from the roasted vegetables then chop them. Cook the pasta as directed. Put the tomato passata into a large pan and add the roasted vegetables, mushrooms, herbs, chilli sauce and black pepper. Cook over a medium heat for 5 minutes then stir in the Mozzarella cheese. Put the pasta on individual plates then spoon the roasted vegetable sauce over the pasta.

SPOTLIGHT   People 'on a diet' usually talk about food constantly and bore their friends and colleagues to distraction. But on The Pyramid Plan, you'll be telling everyone how much better you feel – if they don't beat you to it, telling you how much better you look!

DAY 26

△ Light Meal

POTATO, APPLE AND CASHEW NUT SALAD

300 g (10 oz) potatoes, cooked and cut into small pieces
1 apple, cored and sliced
5 ml (1 tsp) reduced-calorie mayonnaise
10 ml (2 tsp) low-fat natural yogurt
5 ml (1 tsp) chopped fresh mint
50 g (2 oz) cashew nuts

Put the potatoes and apple into a bowl. Mix together the mayonnaise, yogurt and mint then add to the salad, stirring to coat the potatoes and apple. Arrange on individual plates then scatter the cashew nuts on to the salad.

△ Main Meal

PRAWN AND LENTIL CURRY

220 g (8 oz) cooked peeled prawns
420 g (15 oz) tin cooked lentils, drained (if using dried, cook as directed)
1 medium onion, chopped
125 ml (5 fl oz) tomato passata
5 ml (1 tsp) ground coriander
3 ml (1/2 tsp) ground cumin
3 ml (1/2 tsp) ground turmeric
100 g (4 oz) mushrooms, chopped
chilli sauce, to taste
125 g (5 oz) low-fat natural yogurt
freshly ground black pepper and salt

Put the onion and tomato passata into a large pan and cook over a medium heat for 5 minutes. Stir in the ground coriander, cumin and turmeric then add the mushrooms and cook for a further 5 minutes. Add the lentils, chilli sauce to taste, yogurt, black pepper and salt. Finally, add the prawns and heat thoroughly. Serve with basmati rice.

SPOTLIGHT   Every time you have fresh fruit after a meal rather than a dessert, or a glass of mineral water instead of a snack you don't need, you are one step in the right direction of getting into good habits.

DAY 27

△ Light Meal

PROVENÇAL TOASTED SANDWICH

2 × 13 cm (5 inch) wedges of French bread, cut length-ways
1 beef tomato, cut into 8 slices
50 g (2 oz) low-fat cheese, grated
8 black olives
fresh basil leaves

Toast the bread on both sides. Arrange the slices of tomato on the toast and add the grated cheese and olives. Grill until golden. Serve garnished with basil leaves.

△ Main Meal

CHICKEN WITH LEMON AND MINT

2 chicken breast fillets, skin removed, cut into strips
1 red onion, chopped
3 ml (1/2 tsp) grated lemon zest
juice of 1 lemon
10 ml (2 tsp) chopped fresh mint or 5 ml (1 tsp) mint sauce
freshly ground black pepper
2 medium courgettes, sliced
1 medium green pepper, chopped
100 g (4 oz) mushrooms, chopped

Put the chicken and onion into a pan, cover with water and cook over a medium heat for 15 minutes, stirring occasionally. Reduce the liquid to about 15 ml (1 tbsp). Mix together the lemon zest and juice, mint and black pepper and pour over the chicken. Add the courgettes, green pepper and mushrooms, stir thoroughly and cook for a further 5 minutes. Serve with jacket or new potatoes.

SPOTLIGHT Don't let anyone put you off your new lifestyle. You know that exercising regularly and eating healthily make good sense. Ignore the couch potatoes – your new-found energy and vitality speak for themselves.

DAY 28

▲ Light Meal

MUSHROOM FRITTATA

150 g (6 oz) mushrooms, thinly sliced
1 small onion, finely chopped
3 large eggs
freshly ground black pepper and salt
3 ml (1/2 tsp) dried mixed herbs
5 ml (1 tsp) olive oil
2 sprigs fresh parsley

Put the mushrooms and onion into a small pan with a little water and simmer for about 5 minutes, reducing the liquid if necessary. Meanwhile, whisk the eggs with a little water, some freshly ground black pepper and salt. Add the herbs. Heat the olive oil in a small omelette pan and add the eggs, cooking until almost set. Finish cooking under a hot grill. Arrange the mushrooms and onion on the omelette, fold over and cut in half. Serve on individual plates, garnished with a sprig of parsley.

▲ Main Meal

PROVENÇAL FISH

2 × 125 g (5 oz) white fish steaks
2 shallots, finely chopped
1 clove garlic, finely chopped
125 ml (5 fl oz) tomato passata
1 glass red wine
1 small green pepper, diced
1 small red pepper, diced
100 g (4 oz) mushrooms, chopped
5 ml (1 tsp) dried mixed herbs
freshly ground black pepper and salt

Put the shallots and garlic into a pan with the tomato passata and red wine and cook over a medium heat for 5 minutes, stirring occasionally. Add the fish steaks, green and red peppers, mushrooms, herbs, black pepper and salt and cook for a further 10 minutes, adding a little more wine if necessary. Serve with broccoli or spinach and wedges of fresh wholemeal bread.

SPOTLIGHT   When entertaining friends, show how appetising healthy eating can be. Always present food in an attractive way (do this even when it's just for yourself). When you are planning your meal, think about the colours of the foods – simple garnishes such as wedges of lemon or lime add colour to a dish. Your friends will soon be asking for the recipes.

DAY 29

△ Light Meal

HAM, PEACH AND CUCUMBER SALAD

2 slices lean cooked ham
1 peach
wedge of cucumber
10 ml (2 tsp) reduced-
   calorie mayonnaise

10 ml (2 tsp) low-fat natural
   yogurt
5 ml (1 tsp) lemon juice

Mix together the mayonnaise, natural yogurt and lemon juice. Cut the peach and cucumber into small pieces and coat with the mayonnaise mixture. Put the ham on individual plates and spoon the salad on to the ham. Serve with wholemeal bread.

△ Main Meal

SOYA BEAN AND COURGETTE GRATIN

420 g (15 oz) tin cooked
   soya beans, drained (if
   using dried, cook as
   directed)
2 large courgettes, sliced
1 medium onion, chopped
1 clove garlic, finely chopped

4 medium tomatoes,
   chopped
5 ml (1 tsp) dried mixed
   herbs
freshly ground black pepper
100 g (4 oz) low-fat cheese,
   grated

Put the onion, garlic, tomatoes and herbs into a pan with 125 ml (5 fl oz) water, and cook over a medium heat for 5 minutes, stirring occasionally to prevent sticking. Add the courgettes and cook for a further 5 minutes. Add the cooked soya beans and some freshly ground black pepper, then put this mixture into an ovenproof dish. Scatter the grated cheese over the vegetables then bake in a preheated oven, Gas Mark 6 (200°C/400°F), for about 20 minutes until the cheese is golden.

SPOTLIGHT Alcoholic drinks are high in calories. Try sparkling mineral water with ice and lemon instead of an alcoholic aperitif – that's one less already!

DAY 30

△ Light Meal

PRAWN SALAD

150 g (6 oz) cooked peeled
  prawns
10 ml (2 tsp) reduced-calorie
  mayonnaise

5 ml (1 tsp) lemon juice
lettuce leaves
2 tomatoes
wedge of cucumber

Mix the mayonnaise with the lemon juice and coat the prawns
with this mixture. Arrange the lettuce leaves on individual
plates then spoon the prawns on to the lettuce leaves. Slice
the tomatoes and cucumber then arrange alternate slices
around the prawns.

△ Main Meal

STIR-FRY BEEF AND VEGETABLES

220 g (8 oz) lean beef steak
15 ml (1 tbsp) sunflower oil
1 medium carrot, cut into
  julienne strips
1 stick celery, thinly sliced
small piece root ginger,
  peeled and shredded
1 clove garlic, finely chopped

1 small red pepper, diced
50 g (2 oz) mangetout
10 ml (2 tsp) Nam Pla fish
  sauce
5 ml (1 tsp) soy sauce
juice of 1/2 orange
4 spring onions, shredded
freshly ground black pepper

Cut the steak into slivers, 1 × 2.5 cm (½ × 1 inch), as thinly
as possible – this is easier if the meat is put into the freezer for
about 30 minutes before cutting. Heat the oil in a large pan
or wok and add the slivers of beef steak, carrot, celery, ginger
and garlic. Cook for 3–4 minutes, stirring continuously. Add
the red pepper and mangetout then stir in the fish sauce,
soy sauce, soy and orange juice. Finally, add the shredded
spring onions and some freshly ground black pepper. Serve
with brown rice.

SPOTLIGHT   Well done. You're a winner. You should feel pleased with yourself. You have now completed The 30-Day Walkout and The Weight-off and you are well on the way to achieving lifelong health, fitness and weight control. Pat yourself on the back and give yourself a treat!

Part Three

The Pyramid Diet Maintenance Plan

1

Keeping Up A Pyramid
Lifestyle: Six Steps to Success

The following six steps will help you maintain the new level of health and fitness that you have found during The 30-Day Walkout and Weight-loss plan.

△ 1. Fit for Life

Now it's up to you. You started out at your own level and you should now be walking comfortably for 45 minutes at a time. You should be feeling fitter, healthier and more energetic than ever, and be raring to get going with month two. You may have your own target for fitness and weight loss, in which case repeat the plan or adapt it to suit your personal goals. What you now do is up to you. You are an accomplished walker. The road ahead awaits your pleasure.

Your maintenance goal is to perform three to five weekly sessions of aerobic exercise plus two sessions of The Whole Body Workout each week. So either adapt The Walkout as a stand-alone plan or mix 'n' match with cycling, swimming or LI aerobics. You need to continue measuring your target heart rate by following the advice on page 53 (Target Heart Rate Made Simple) or alternatively use the Borg Scale of Perceived Exertion on page 51 to monitor your exercise intensity. Or use the Talk Test (see page 28) to ensure that you are not working at too high a level. Remember to warm up and do your Quick and Post Stretches.

So long as you are performing this minimum amount of

exercise, you will be doing sufficient to maintain aerobic fitness and maintain your 'reasonable weight' once you have achieved it. As you will have discovered, exercise is about much more than fitness and weight loss. It's about feeling good about yourself, increased self-confidence and stress release. And you continue exercising because you can't do without this experience in your life.

△ 2. Tips For Healthy Eating

- △   Follow the guidelines of The Healthy Eating Pyramid.
- △   Eat wholefoods – foods which have nothing added and nothing taken away.
- △   Eat more fresh foods, especially fruit and vegetables, and less processed foods – nutrients are lost in processing.
- △   Eat more complex carbohydrates and less foods which are high in fat, sugar, salt and additives.
- △   Eat foods in season.
- △   Bake, steam, poach or grill foods instead of frying.
- △   Eat more grains, pulses, fish and white meat; if you eat red meat, eat lean cuts.
- △   Eat slowly and in moderate quantities.
- △   Look at labels on tinned or other processed food for the fat, sugar and salt content.
- △   Make gradual changes – small steps in the right direction. You will soon see an improvement in your general health and well-being.

△ 3. Substitutes

Use	*Instead of*
skimmed or semi-skimmed milk	full-fat milk
low-fat natural yogurt or reduced fat cream	cream, single or double

wholemeal bread	white bread
tomato- or yogurt-based sauces	cheese- or cream-based sauces
lemon juice, lime juice or reduced-calorie mayonnaise	French dressing or mayonnaise
herbs as flavouring	salt
fresh fruit or low-fat natural yogurt	desserts and puddings
crudités or fresh fruit	biscuits, cakes and other snacks
mineral water or low-alcohol drinks	alcoholic drinks
fresh fruit or vegetable juices	tea and coffee

△ 4. Identifying Fat and Fibre in Foods

The following lists show the relative fat and fibre content of various foods. They should help you identify which foods to decrease (fat) and which foods to increase (fibre) as part of a balanced, nutrious diet.

△ Fat

VERY HIGH   (over 25 g per 100 g): chocolate, biscuits, cakes, pastries, cream, butter, cheese, lard, oils, fried foods, mayonnaise, nuts.

HIGH   (over 15 g per 100 g): bacon, grilled sausages, roast duck, tinned fish in oil, avocado pears, chips, pancakes, toffees, doughnuts.

MEDIUM   (over 6 g per 100 g): roast beef, lamb, pork, roast chicken and turkey (with skin), Greek yogurt, eggs, herring, kipper.

LOW   (under 6 g per 100 g): chicken and turkey cooked

without fat, steamed cod and haddock, fresh tuna, prawns, wholemeal bread, skimmed or semi-skimmed milk.

△ Fibre

VERY HIGH   (over 10 g per 100 g): peas, red kidney beans, dried apricots and prunes, wheatbran.

HIGH   (over 6 g per 100 g): baked beans, spinach, black-currants, raspberries, dried raisins and sultanas, wholemeal bread.

MEDIUM   (over 2 g per 100 g): broad beans, French beans, cabbage, leeks, apples, bananas, pears, white bread.

LOW   (under 2 g per 100 g): celery, cauliflower, cucumber, lettuce, grapes, peaches, oranges, melon.

△ 5. Stock Check

Here are some shopping lists for The Pyramid Plan.

△ Groceries

Bread, rice, pasta, lentils, beans (baked, red kidney, soya, white haricot), petits pois, chick peas, couscous, tuna in brine, chopped tomatoes, tomato purée, fresh herbs, dried mixed herbs, spices (ground coriander, cumin, turmeric, cinnamon), chilli sauce, Nam Pla fish sauce, sultanas, almonds, walnuts, chestnuts, seeds (pumpkin, sunflower, sesame), black peppercorns, sea salt.

△ Fruit and Vegetables

Apples, bananas, pears, melon, grapes, pineapple, lemons, limes, oranges, grapefruit, paw paw, strawberries, raspberries, rhubarb, blueberries, kiwi fruit, apricots, peaches, nectarines, tomatoes, onions, garlic, mushrooms, red peppers, green peppers, carrots, potatoes, broccoli, spinach, cabbage, Brussels sprouts, cauliflower, peas, beans, celery, leeks, parsnips, sweetcorn, turnips, swede, lettuce, watercress, cucumber.

△ Fish, Poultry, Meat, Dairy Products

Cod, haddock, salmon, tuna, hake, monkfish, herrings, mackerel, prawns, crab; chicken fillets, turkey fillets, ground lean turkey, beef, lamb, lean red meat, pork, venison, guinea fowl; skimmed or semi-skimmed milk, eggs, low-fat natural yogurt, low-fat cheese.

△ Fats and Oils

Olive oil, sunflower oil, low-fat margarine.

△ 6. Keeping It Up!

Keeping up The Pyramid Plan is all a question of following the 3Cs – Commitment, Consistency and Confirmation.

△ Commitment

This fires your enthusiasm, gets you on your feet, and keeps you motivated when the going gets tough. In the same way that exercise increases physical stamina, commitment builds mental stamina that gives you the strength to carry on.

△ Consistency

This is all about regular habits – building a long-term routine that is enjoyable and fun to do. You begin with small habits – cycling to work, walking on a weekend, cutting down on fat and processed foods – and you build them into big habits which become as automatic as cleaning your teeth or having a shower.

△ Confirmation

This is a record of your commitment and consistency. Keeping an exercise log or food diary and recording each day's activities helps you measure your progress and it helps keep you motivated. It can help you plan your exercise and meals in advance. Scheduling your exercise and meals with clear objectives will ensure that you arrive at your goal – success!

2

The Pyramid Diet Maintenance Plan Recipes

The following recipes continue the nutritional theme of The Pyramid 30-Day Weight-loss Plan. They allow you to work out your own maintenance plan based on your personal tastes and nutritional needs. Choose your own favourites, and mix 'n' match recipes for variety and enjoyment.

△ Light Meals

TUNA, BROCCOLI AND WALNUT SALAD

220 g (8 oz) tin tuna in brine, drained
1 small head of broccoli
2 spring onions, cut into small pieces

5 ml (1 tsp) white wine vinegar
15 ml (1 tbsp) freshly squeezed orange juice
10 ml (2 tsp) chopped walnuts
freshly ground black pepper

Cut the broccoli into florets and shred the stem. Put into a pan with some boiling water and simmer for 5 minutes then drain thoroughly. Flake the tuna then mix with the broccoli and spring onions and arrange on individual plates. Mix together the wine vinegar and orange juice and spoon over the salad. Add the chopped walnuts and freshly ground black pepper.

SMOKED COD AND LEEK SALAD

150 g (6 oz) smoked cod
2 medium leeks, cut into
   halves lengthways and
   cleaned

10 ml (2 tsp) white wine
   vinegar
5 ml (1 tsp) olive oil
freshly ground black pepper

Poach the smoked cod in some water or a mixture of milk and water and in another pan simmer the leeks in boiling water for about 8 minutes. Drain and leave to cool. Arrange the leeks on individual plates then flake the fish and put on to the leeks. Mix together the wine vinegar and olive oil, spoon over the salad then add freshly ground black pepper.

PAW PAW AND PRAWN SALAD

1 paw paw
150 g (6 oz) cooked peeled
   prawns

2 small spring onions
juice of 1 lime
freshly ground black pepper

Cut the paw paw in half, spoon out the seeds then peel the skin from the fruit. Cut the paw paw into slices and arrange on individual plates. Finely slice the spring onions and mix with the prawns and lime juice. Arrange on the paw paw and add freshly ground black pepper.

SPICY CRAB AND PAW PAW SALAD

1 paw paw
220 g (8 oz) tin white crab
   meat
1 small green pepper
1 small red onion

chilli sauce, to taste
juice of 1 lime
lettuce leaves
freshly ground black pepper

Cut the paw paw in half, spoon out the seeds then peel the skin from the fruit. Cut into cubes. Finely chop the green pepper and red onion then mix with the paw paw and crab meat. Mix the chilli sauce and lime juice and gently stir into the salad. Put the lettuce leaves on individual plates and arrange the salad on the lettuce. Add some freshly ground black pepper.

WARM SALAD WITH PRAWNS

150 g (6 oz) cooked peeled prawns
5 ml (1 tsp) olive oil
1 shallot, finely chopped
5 ml (1 tsp) white wine vinegar
5 ml (1 tsp) lime juice
lettuce leaves
5 ml (1 tsp) chopped fresh dill
freshly ground black pepper
2 lime wedges

Heat the olive oil gently in a small pan and add the chopped shallot. Cook for 5 minutes, stirring occasionally. Add the prawns, white wine vinegar and lime juice and stir until heated through. Arrange the lettuce leaves on individual plates and spoon over the prawns and warm vinaigrette. Add the chopped fresh dill and some freshly ground black pepper, and garnish with a wedge of lime.

WARM SALAD WITH BACON

2 bacon rashers, cut into strips
5 ml (1 tsp) sunflower oil
1 shallot, finely chopped
5 ml (1 tsp) white wine vinegar
5 ml (1 tsp) lemon juice
lettuce leaves
freshly ground black pepper
2 lemon wedges

Heat the sunflower oil in a small pan and add the chopped shallot and pieces of bacon. Cook for about 5 minutes, stirring to prevent sticking. Add the white wine vinegar and lemon juice and heat through. Arrange the lettuce leaves on individual plates and spoon over the bacon, shallot and warm vinaigrette. Add some freshly ground black pepper and garnish with a wedge of lemon.

FETA AND BEAN SALAD

75 g (3 oz) feta cheese
150 g (6 oz) cooked white
    haricot beans
2 medium tomatoes
wedge of cucumber

5 ml (1 tsp) olive oil
5 ml (1 tsp) balsamic vinegar
5 ml (1 tsp) chopped fresh
    dill
freshly ground black pepper

Slice the tomatoes and cucumber and arrange on individual plates. Mix together the olive oil, balsamic vinegar and dill and gently stir in the beans to coat with the vinaigrette. Spoon on to the tomatoes and cucumber. Slice the feta cheese and arrange on the salad then add some freshly ground black pepper.

WATERCRESS, TUNA AND PEAR SALAD

bunch of watercress
220 g (8 oz) tin tuna in brine,
    drained
2 medium pears, quartered,
    cored and cut into small
    pieces

10 ml (2 tsp) reduced-calorie
    mayonnaise
10 ml (2 tsp) low-fat natural
    yogurt
5 ml (1 tsp) lemon juice
freshly ground black pepper
2 lemon wedges

Arrange the watercress on individual plates. Mix together the tuna, pears, mayonnaise, yogurt and lemon juice then spoon on to the watercress. Add some freshly ground black pepper and garnish with a wedge of lemon.

SPICY SALAD

wedge of red cabbage, finely
    sliced
1 stick celery, finely sliced
1 small red pepper, diced
1 medium tomato, diced

10 ml (2 tsp) lime juice
5 ml (1 tsp) soy sauce
chilli sauce, to taste
25 g (1 oz) pine nuts, toasted
freshly ground black pepper

Put the red cabbage, celery, red pepper and tomato into a
bowl. Mix together the lime juice, soy sauce and chilli sauce
and add to the salad, mixing well. Arrange on individual
plates, scatter the toasted pine nuts on to the salad and add
some freshly ground black pepper.

MAGREB SALAD

150g (6 oz) couscous
1 large courgette, thinly
    sliced
1 small green pepper, diced
1 medium tomato, diced
juice of 1 lemon

10 ml (2 tsp) chopped fresh
    mint
5 ml (1 tsp) sunflower oil
freshly ground black pepper
    and salt
2 lemon wedges

Prepare the couscous as directed on the packet then leave
to cool. Put in a bowl with the courgette, green pepper
and tomato. Mix together the lemon juice, mint, sunflower
oil, black pepper and salt then add to the salad and mix
well. Serve on individual plates and garnish with a wedge
of lemon.

MANGETOUT AND EGG SALAD

100 g (4 oz) mangetout, lightly
  cooked
2 eggs, hard-boiled and
  quartered
lettuce leaves
10 ml (2 tsp) olive oil

5 ml (1 tsp) white wine
  vinegar
small piece fresh ginger,
  peeled and shredded
freshly ground black pepper
2 lemon wedges

Arrange the lettuce leaves on individual plates then add the
mangetout and egg quarters. Mix the olive oil, white wine
vinegar and shredded ginger and spoon over the salad.
Add some freshly ground black pepper and garnish with
lemon wedges.

AVOCADO AND KIWI FRUIT SALAD

1 small avocado, halved,
  peeled and cut into pieces
2 kiwi fruit, peeled and sliced
lettuce leaves
5 ml (1 tsp) lemon juice

5 ml (1 tsp) white wine
  vinegar
3 ml (1/2 tsp) mustard
freshly ground black pepper
2 lemon wedges

Put the lettuce leaves on individual plates then arrange the
avocado pieces and kiwi fruit slices on the lettuce. Mix the
lemon juice, white wine vinegar and mustard then spoon
over the salad. Add some freshly ground black pepper and
garnish with lemon wedges.

PEPPER AND PRAWN SALAD

1 medium red pepper
1 medium green pepper
100 g (4 oz) cooked peeled
  prawns

10 ml (2 tsp) reduced-calorie
  mayonnaise
5 ml (1 tsp) lemon juice
freshly ground black pepper

Cut each pepper lengthways into four pieces and remove
the seeds. Grill under a medium heat for about 5 minutes
on each side. Leave to cool then peel the skin from the

peppers. Arrange two pieces of red and two pieces of green pepper on individual plates. Mix the mayonnaise with the lemon juice then gently stir in the prawns. Spoon on to the peppers and add some freshly ground black pepper.

MEXICAN SALAD

100 g (4 oz) cooked peeled prawns
100 g (4 oz) cooked crab meat
10 ml (2 tsp) lime juice
5 ml (1 tsp) reduced-calorie mayonnaise

chilli sauce, to taste
1 shallot, finely chopped
1 small green pepper, diced
wedge of cucumber, diced
2 large iceberg lettuce leaves
freshly ground black pepper
2 lime wedges

Mix together the lime juice, mayonnaise and chilli sauce in a bowl. Gently stir in the prawns, crab meat, shallot, green pepper and cucumber. Put the lettuce leaves on individual plates then spoon the salad into the lettuce leaves. Add some freshly ground black pepper and garnish with the lime wedges.

SMOKED MACKEREL, CELERY AND ALMOND SALAD

1 smoked mackerel fillet, skin removed
1 stick celery, finely sliced
50 g (2 oz) flaked almonds

10 ml (2 tsp) reduced-calorie mayonnaise
5 ml (1 tsp) lemon juice
freshly ground black pepper

Flake the smoked mackerel fillet then mix with the celery and almonds. Mix together the mayonnaise and lemon juice then coat the salad with the dressing. Arrange on individual plates then add some freshly ground black pepper.

CROQUE MONSIEUR

4 slices bread
75 g (3 oz) low-fat cheese, grated

5 ml (1 tsp) mustard
2 slices lean ham
frisée or other lettuce leaf

Toast the bread on both sides. Arrange the grated cheese on two of the slices and put under the grill until golden. Meanwhile, put mustard on the other two slices of toast and add the ham. Put the slices of toast with cheese on the slices with ham and cut into four diagonally. Arrange the frisée on individual plates and add the pieces of croque monsieur.

CROQUE MADAME

4 slices bread
75 g (3 oz) low-fat cheese, grated
10 ml (2 tsp) fruit pickle

1 cooked chicken breast fillet, skin removed and sliced
radicchio or other lettuce leaf

Toast the bread on both sides. Arrange the grated cheese on two of the slices and put under the grill until golden. Meanwhile, put fruit pickle on the other two slices of toast and add the chicken. Put the slices of toast with cheese on the slices with chicken and cut into four diagonally. Arrange the radicchio on individual plates and add the pieces of croque madame.

TRICOLORE SALAD

1 small avocado
juice of 1/2 lime
1 beef tomato
1/2 Italian Mozzarella cheese

freshly ground black pepper
fresh basil leaves
2 lime wedges

Peel the avocado and cut into slices. Arrange on individual plates then pour the lime juice on the avocado. Slice the tomato and Mozzarella cheese and arrange on the avocado slices. Add some freshly ground black pepper and garnish with basil leaves and lime wedges.

PRAWN AND MELON SALAD

100 g (4 oz) cooked peeled
  prawns
large wedge of melon, seeds
  and skin removed, diced
2 spring onions, finely
  chopped
8 cherry tomatoes, halved

small wedge of cucumber,
  diced
juice of 1/2 lemon
10 ml (2 tsp) chopped fresh
  chives
freshly ground black pepper

Put the prawns, melon, spring onions, tomatoes and cucumber into a bowl and gently mix. Arrange on individual plates then add the lemon juice, chives and freshly ground black pepper.

SALAMI AND CASHEW NUT SALAD

4 thin slices salami, cut into
  strips
50 g (2 oz) natural cashew
  nuts, halved

radicchio or other salad
  leaves
4 black olives
2 lemon wedges
freshly ground black pepper

Arrange the salad leaves on individual plates then add the salami. Scatter the cashew nuts over the salad and garnish with black olives and lemon wedges. Add some freshly ground black pepper.

ANTIPASTO

2 slices Parma ham
4 thin slices salami
1 medium tomato, sliced
8 black olives

fresh basil leaves
2 lemon wedges
freshly ground black pepper

Put the Parma ham and salami on individual plates. Add the slices of tomato and black olives then garnish with basil leaves and lemon wedges. Add some freshly ground black pepper.

FLORENTINE EGG SALAD

220g (8 oz) spinach leaves
2 hard-boiled eggs, quartered
5 ml (1 tsp) balsamic vinegar

5 ml (1 tsp) lemon juice
freshly ground black pepper
8 black olives

Wilt the spinach leaves by putting them in boiling water for about 1 minute, then drain and squeeze excess water from the leaves. Leave to cool then arrange on individual plates. Mix together the balsamic vinegar and lemon juice and spoon on to the spinach. Add the egg quarters and some freshly ground black pepper, and garnish with black olives.

FRISÉE AND PARMA HAM SALAD

frisée lettuce leaves
4 slices Parma ham, cut into
    strips
5 ml (1 tsp) olive oil

5 ml (1 tsp) lemon juice
8 button mushrooms, thinly
    sliced
freshly ground black pepper

Mix together the olive oil and lemon juice and coat the mushrooms with this dressing. Arrange the frisée on individual plates and spoon the mushrooms on to the frisée. Scatter the strips of Parma ham on to the salad and add some freshly ground black pepper.

TOMATO, KIWI FRUIT AND CUCUMBER SALAD

2 medium tomatoes, sliced
2 kiwi fruit, peeled and sliced
wedge of cucumber, cut into
    small pieces

75 g (3 oz) low-fat natural
    yogurt
10 ml (2 tsp) lemon juice
freshly ground black pepper

Mix together the yogurt and lemon juice and stir in the cucumber. Arrange alternate slices of tomato and kiwi fruit in a circle on individual plates. Spoon the cucumber mixture into the middle of the salad. Add some freshly ground black pepper.

△ **Main Meals**

△ Vegetarian

PASTA WITH ASPARAGUS AND PINE NUTS

150 g (6 oz) pasta
220 g (8 oz) asparagus
1 medium onion, chopped
10 ml (2 tsp) Nam Pla fish
    sauce
100 ml (4 fl oz) low-fat single
    cream

50 g (2 oz) pine nuts
10 ml (2 tsp) fresh basil, torn
    into pieces
freshly ground black pepper
fresh Parmesan cheese, to
    garnish

Cook the pasta as directed. Cut the woody ends from the asparagus and discard then cut the rest of the asparagus into 2.5 cm (1 inch) pieces. Put the chopped onion into a medium saucepan and cover with cold water. Bring to the boil then simmer over a medium heat for 5 minutes. Add the asparagus and simmer for a further 5 minutes. Reduce the liquid to about 10 ml (2 tsp). Stir in the fish sauce and cream and warm through. Add the pine nuts, fresh basil and black pepper and stir gently. Put the pasta on to individual plates and spoon over the sauce. Garnish with some slivers of fresh Parmesan cheese.

PENNE SICILIANA

150 g (6 oz) penne
2 shallots, finely chopped
1 clove garlic, finely chopped
1 medium aubergine, cut
    into 1 cm (1/2 inch) pieces
420g (15 oz) tin chopped
    tomatoes

100 g (4 oz) mushrooms, cut
    into small pieces
1 small red pepper, diced
10 ml (2 tsp) fresh basil, torn
    into pieces
1/2 Italian Mozzarella
    cheese, cubed
freshly ground black pepper

Cook the penne as directed. Put the shallots, garlic, aubergine and chopped tomatoes into a pan and cook over a medium heat for 10 minutes. Add the mushrooms and red pepper and cook for a further 5 minutes. Add the basil, Mozzarella cheese and some freshly ground black pepper and stir well. Serve the penne on individual plates with the sauce spooned over the pasta.

TAGLIATELLE PRIMAVERA

150 g (6 oz) tagliatelle
1 small onion, finely chopped
1 stick celery, finely chopped
1 medium carrot, diced
1 medium courgette, diced
1 small red pepper, diced
4 asparagus spears, cut into
    2.5 cm (1 inch) pieces
    (discard woody end)

125 ml (5 fl oz) low-fat single
    cream
10 ml (2 tsp) chopped fresh
    flat-leaf parsley
10 ml (2 tsp) freshly grated
    Parmesan cheese
freshly ground black pepper
    and salt

Cook the tagliatelle as directed. Put the onion, celery and carrot into a pan with 300 ml (10 fl oz) water and cook over a medium heat for 5 minutes. Add the courgette, red pepper and asparagus and cook for a further 5 minutes or until the vegetables are tender. Reduce the liquid to about 30 ml (2 tbsp). Stir in the cream, parsley, Parmesan cheese, some freshly ground black pepper and salt and heat thoroughly. Serve the tagliatelle on individual plates with the sauce spooned over the pasta.

SPICY RICE WITH GRILLED VEGETABLES

150 g (6 oz) long-grain brown
    rice
1 medium onion, peeled and
    cut into quarters
1 green pepper, cut into 2.5
    cm (1 inch) pieces
1 red pepper, cut into 2.5 cm
    (1 inch) pieces
1 medium courgette, cut in
    half lengthways

2 large mushrooms
300 ml (10 fl oz) tomato
    passata
5 ml (1 tsp) ground
    coriander
3 ml (1/2 tsp) ground
    cinnamon
chilli sauce, to taste
freshly ground black pepper
2 lemon wedges

Cook the rice as directed. Meanwhile, cook the onion, green and red peppers, courgette and mushrooms under a preheated grill for about 8 minutes, turning once. Put the tomato passata, coriander, cinnamon, chilli sauce to taste and some freshly ground black pepper into a pan and heat thoroughly, stirring to prevent sticking. Cut the courgette and mushrooms into small pieces and add to the sauce along with the other vegetables. Drain the rice and arrange on individual plates. Spoon the sauce over the rice and serve garnished with lemon wedges.

WILD RICE WITH MUSHROOMS

150 g (6 oz) wild rice or wild
   and long-grain rice, mixed
300 g (10 oz) mushrooms
   (use a variety of types if
   possible)
50 g (2 oz) dried mushrooms,
   soaked in 125 ml (5 fl oz)
   water

2 shallots, finely chopped
1 clove garlic, finely chopped
125 ml (5 fl oz) tomato
   passata
125 ml (5 fl oz) red wine
freshly ground black pepper
   and salt
fresh basil leaves

Cook the rice as directed. Meanwhile, put the shallots, garlic and all the mushrooms into a pan with the water from the dried mushrooms and cook over a medium heat for about 8 minutes, stirring occasionally and adding more water if necessary. There should be about 15 ml (1 tbsp) reduced liquid after cooking. Add the tomato passata, red wine, some freshly ground black pepper and salt and heat thoroughly. Drain the rice and stir into the sauce. Serve garnished with basil leaves.

△ Fish and Seafood

SALMON FLORENTINE

2 × 125 g (5 oz) skinless fillets of salmon
220 g (8 oz) fresh spinach
10 ml (2 tsp) olive oil

10 ml (2 tsp) Nam Pla fish sauce
freshly ground black pepper

Heat the olive oil gently in a small pan and cook the salmon fillets for about 8 minutes, turning once or twice. Meanwhile, put the spinach in a large pan with a little water and cook over a medium heat for 2–3 minutes. Drain thoroughly then return to the pan. Add the Nam Pla fish sauce to the spinach. Arrange the spinach on individual plates and put the salmon fillet on the spinach. Add some freshly ground black pepper.

SALMON WITH PINE NUTS

2 × 125 g (5 oz) skinless fillets of salmon
2 shallots, chopped
420 g (15 oz) tin chopped tomatoes
10 ml (2 tsp) Nam Pla fish sauce

10 ml (2 tsp) chopped fresh flat-leaf parsley
freshly ground black pepper
50 g (2 oz) sultanas
50 g (2 oz) pine nuts

Put the shallots and the chopped tomatoes into a medium pan and cook for about 8 minutes. Stir in the fish sauce, parsley and black pepper then add the salmon fillets. Simmer for a further 8 minutes, adding the sultanas for the last 2 minutes. Meanwhile, lightly toast the pine nuts. Arrange the salmon fillets and the sauce on individual plates then garnish with the pine nuts.

TANDOORI FISH

2 × 125 g (5 oz) skinless
 fillets of cod
1 clove garlic, finely chopped
5 ml (1 tsp) ground
 coriander
3 ml (1/2 tsp) ground cumin
3 ml (1/2 tsp) ground
 turmeric

few drops of chilli sauce
125 g (5 oz) low-fat natural
 yogurt
15 ml (1 tbsp) lemon juice
freshly ground black pepper
 and salt
lettuce leaves, shredded
2 lemon wedges

Mix together the garlic, coriander, cumin, turmeric, chilli sauce, yogurt, lemon juice, black pepper and salt. Put the fish fillets into this marinade and leave in the fridge for at least 30 minutes – if possible, for 2 or 3 hours – turning occasionally. Take the fish fillets out of the marinade and put on a wire rack over a baking tray. Bake in a preheated oven, Gas Mark 6 (200°C/400°F), for about 25 minutes. Serve on individual plates, garnished with shredded lettuce and lemon wedges.

GRILLED SARDINES WITH LENTILS

6–8 fresh sardines, gutted
 and cleaned
420 g (15 oz) tin cooked
 lentils, drained (if using
 dried, cook as directed)
2 shallots, finely chopped
1 clove garlic, finely chopped

2 medium tomatoes,
 chopped
5 ml (1 tsp) dried mixed
 herbs
freshly ground black pepper
chilli sauce, to taste

Grill the sardines for about 8 minutes, turning to cook evenly. Meanwhile, put the shallots, garlic, tomatoes, herbs and black pepper into a pan with a little water and cook over a medium heat for 5 minutes, stirring occasionally. Stir in the cooked lentils and chilli sauce and heat thoroughly. Serve the lentils on individual plates and arrange the grilled sardines on the lentils.

MONKFISH NANTAIS

2 × 125 g (5 oz) fillets of
  monkfish
2 shallots, finely chopped
100 g (4 oz) petits pois
100 g (4 oz) white
  mushrooms, thinly sliced

3 ml (1/2 tsp) mustard
10 ml (2 tsp) Nam Pla fish
  sauce
125 ml (5 fl oz) low-fat single
  cream
freshly ground black pepper

Put the chopped shallots and petits pois into a pan with
300 ml (10 fl oz) water and cook over a medium heat for
5 minutes. Stir in the mushrooms then put the monkfish
on to the vegetables. Cover the pan and cook for a further
5 minutes. Reduce the liquid to about 30 ml (2 tbsp). Add
the mustard, fish sauce, cream and some freshly ground black
pepper, and heat thoroughly, stirring gently.

FISH KEBABS

300 g (10 oz) skinless fillets
  of haddock, cubed
4 bay leaves
juice of 1/2 lemon
5 ml (1 tsp) ground
  coriander
freshly ground black pepper

1 medium red onion, cut into
  wedges
1 medium green pepper, cut
  into large pieces
2 medium tomatoes,
  quartered

Put the cubes of fish and the bay leaves into a bowl. Mix
together the lemon juice, ground coriander and freshly
ground black pepper then pour over the fish. Cover and
leave to marinate in the fridge for at least 30 minutes – if
possible, for 2 or 3 hours – turning occasionally. Arrange
the fish, bay leaves, onion, green pepper and tomatoes on
skewers then grill the kebabs under a preheated grill for
about 10 minutes, turning to cook evenly.

FISH À LA GRECQUE

300 g (10 oz) skinless fillets
  of white fish, cut into large
  pieces
10 ml (2 tsp) olive oil
1 medium onion, sliced
1 clove garlic, chopped

2 medium tomatoes, skinned
  and chopped
juice of 1/2 lemon
15 ml (1 tbsp) chopped fresh
  parsley
freshly ground black pepper
  and salt

Heat the olive oil in a pan and cook the onion and garlic over a medium heat for 5 minutes, stirring occasionally. Add the tomatoes, lemon juice, parsley, black pepper and salt and cook for a further 5 minutes, adding a little water if too thick. Put the fish in an ovenproof baking dish then pour over the sauce. Bake in a preheated oven, Gas Mark 6 (200°C/400°F), for about 20 minutes.

HOT SPICY FISH

300 g (10 oz) skinless fillets
  of white fish, cut into large
  pieces
10 ml (2 tsp) olive oil
1 medium onion, chopped
1 clove garlic, chopped
1 medium red pepper, diced
25 g (1 oz) almonds,
  chopped

juice of 1 lemon
5 ml (1 tsp) Nam Pla fish
  sauce
15 ml (1 tbsp) chopped fresh
  coriander
3 ml (1/2 tsp) ground
  cinnamon
3 ml (1/2 tsp) cayenne
  pepper

Heat the olive oil in a pan and cook the onion and garlic over a medium heat for 5 minutes. Put the fish in an ovenproof baking dish and add the onion and garlic and also the red pepper and almonds. Mix the remaining ingredients together and add a little water to make a sauce consistency. Pour over the fish and bake in a preheated oven, Gas Mark 6 (200°C/400°F), for about 20 minutes.

PRAWN BROCHETTES

300 g (10 oz) cooked peeled
  tiger prawns
juice of 1/2 lime
5 ml (1 tsp) soy sauce
5 ml (1 tsp) clear honey

3 ml (1/2 tsp) dried mixed
  herbs
freshly ground black pepper
2 medium courgettes, cut
  into wedges
8 cherry tomatoes

Mix together the lime juice, soy sauce, honey, herbs and black pepper and put the prawns into this marinade. Leave in the fridge for at least 30 minutes – if possible, 2 or 3 hours – turning occasionally. Arrange the prawns on skewers with the courgettes and tomatoes and cook under a hot grill for about 10 minutes, turning to cook evenly.

VENETIAN PRAWNS

300 g (10 oz) cooked peeled
  prawns
2 shallots, finely chopped
1 clove garlic, finely chopped
10 ml (2 tsp) olive oil
300 ml (10 fl oz) tomato
  passata

100 g (4 oz) mushrooms,
  sliced
1 medium courgette, grated
15 ml (1 tbsp) chopped fresh
  parsley
10 ml (2 tsp) Nam Pla fish
  sauce
freshly ground black pepper

Put the shallots and garlic into a pan with the olive oil and cook over a medium heat for 5 minutes, stirring to prevent sticking. Add the tomato passata, mushrooms, courgette, parsley and fish sauce and cook for a further 5 minutes. Stir in the prawns and some freshly ground black pepper and heat thoroughly.

PASTA VONGOLE

150 g (6 oz) pasta
300 g (10 oz) tin baby clams
2 shallots, finely chopped
1 clove garlic, finely chopped
420 g (15 oz) tin chopped
   tomatoes

100 g (4 oz) mushrooms,
   sliced
10 ml (2 tsp) Nam Pla fish
   sauce
5 ml (1 tsp) dried mixed
   herbs
freshly ground black pepper

Cook the pasta as directed. Put the shallots, garlic and chopped tomatoes into a pan and cook over a medium heat for 5 minutes. Add the mushrooms, fish sauce, herbs and black pepper and cook for a further 5 minutes. Drain the liquid from the clams then add the clams to the sauce and heat thoroughly. Serve the pasta on individual plates with the clam sauce poured over.

CALAMARI LIVORNESE

2 large or 8 baby squid,
   cleaned and cut into rings
2 shallots, finely chopped
1 clove garlic, finely chopped
300 ml (10 fl oz) tomato
   passata
1 glass red wine

100 g (4 oz) small
   mushrooms, finely sliced
10 ml (2 tsp) Nam Pla fish
   sauce
5 ml (1 tsp) dried mixed
   herbs
freshly ground black pepper

Put the shallots, garlic, tomato passata and red wine into a pan and cook over a medium heat for 5 minutes, stirring occasionally. Add the squid, mushrooms, fish sauce, herbs and black pepper and cook for a further 5 minutes, adding a little more wine if necessary. Serve on individual plates with rice.

△ Poultry and Game

CHICKEN À LA NORMANDE

2 chicken breast fillets, skin
  removed
2 shallots, finely chopped
300 ml (10 fl oz) dry cider
100 g (4 oz) mushrooms,
  sliced

10 ml (2 tsp) chopped fresh
  tarragon
125 ml (5 fl oz) low-fat single
  cream
freshly ground black pepper

Put the chicken, shallots and cider into a pan, cover and
cook for 20–25 minutes. Add the mushrooms and tarragon
and cook for a further 5 minutes. Reduce the liquid to about
15 ml (1 tbsp) then add the cream and some freshly ground
black pepper and heat thoroughly.

CHICKEN WITH RED AND GREEN PEPPERS

2 chicken breast fillets, skin
  removed, cut into bite-size
  pieces
1 small red pepper, cut into
  strips
1 small green pepper, cut
  into strips
1 medium onion, chopped

420 g (15 oz) tin chopped
  tomatoes
100 g (4 oz) mushrooms,
  chopped
5 ml (1 tsp) mustard
5 ml (1 tsp) paprika
10 ml (2 tsp) chopped fresh
  flat-leaf parsley
freshly ground black pepper

Put the chicken, onion and chopped tomatoes into a large
saucepan and cook over a medium heat for about 15 minutes,
stirring occasionally. Add the red and green peppers, mushrooms, mustard, paprika, parsley and black pepper and cook
for a further 5 minutes.

CHINESE KEBABS

2 chicken breast fillets, skin removed, cut into bite-size pieces
1 medium red onion, cut into wedges
1 small green pepper, cut into large pieces
1 small red pepper, cut into large pieces
100 g (4 oz) small mushrooms

30 ml (2 tbsp) soy sauce
10 ml (2 tsp) white wine vinegar
10 ml (2 tsp) fresh orange juice
10 ml (2 tsp) clear honey
small piece fresh root ginger, peeled and shredded
freshly ground black pepper

Arrange the chicken, onion, green and red peppers and mushrooms on skewers and put into a shallow dish. Mix together all the remaining ingredients and pour over the kebabs. Leave to marinate in the fridge for at least 30 minutes – if possible, for 2 or 3 hours – turning occasionally. Grill the kebabs under a preheated grill for about 15 minutes, turning to cook evenly. Meanwhile, put the remaining marinade in a small pan and simmer until reduced. Pour over the kebabs to serve.

CHICKEN WITH SULTANAS AND ALMONDS

2 chicken breast fillets, skin removed, cut into bite-size pieces
150 g (6 oz) long-grain rice
10 ml (2 tsp) sunflower oil
1 medium onion, chopped
1 glass white wine

juice of 1/2 lemon
freshly ground black pepper and salt
25 g (1 oz) flaked almonds
50 g (2 oz) sultanas
2 lemon wedges

Cook the rice as directed. Meanwhile, heat the oil in a large saucepan then add the onion and pieces of chicken. Cook over a medium heat for about 20 minutes, stirring occasionally, and adding the white wine after about 10 minutes. Drain the cooked rice then add to the chicken.

Add the lemon juice, black pepper and salt, flaked almonds and sultanas and stir to amalgamate all ingredients. Serve on individual plates, garnished with a wedge of lemon.

COQ AU VIN

2 chicken breast fillets, skin removed, cut into bite-size pieces
1 medium onion, chopped
1 clove garlic, finely chopped
2 medium carrots, sliced
250 ml (9 fl oz) red wine
1 stick celery, thinly sliced
100 g (4 oz) mushrooms, chopped
5 ml (1 tsp) dried mixed herbs
freshly ground black pepper

Put the chicken, onion, garlic, carrots and red wine into a large pan and cook over a medium heat for about 20 minutes, stirring occasionally. Add the celery, mushrooms, herbs and black pepper and cook for a further 5 minutes, adding more wine or a little water if necessary.

CHICKEN WITH ALMOND AND POMEGRANATE SAUCE

2 chicken breast fillets, skin removed
10 ml (2 tsp) sunflower oil
1 pomegranate
125 ml (5 fl oz) white wine
50 g (2 oz) ground almonds
freshly ground black pepper and salt

Heat the oil in a pan and cook the chicken breast fillets for 5 minutes on each side until light golden brown. Meanwhile, cut the pomegranate in half and scoop out the red seeds, reserving any juice. Add the white wine, ground almonds, pomegranate seeds and juice, freshly ground black pepper and salt to the chicken. Cover and simmer for 15–20 minutes, stirring occasionally to prevent sticking. Serve with rice.

TURKEY LOMBATTINI

2 × 125 g (5 oz) turkey breast fillets
100 g (4 oz) small mushrooms, thinly sliced
1 glass white wine
10 ml (2 tsp) lemon juice
5 ml (1 tsp) mustard
chilli sauce, to taste
5 ml (1 tsp) dried mixed herbs
freshly ground black pepper

Put the turkey and mushrooms into an ovenproof dish. Mix together the white wine, lemon juice, mustard, chilli sauce, herbs and black pepper and pour over the turkey and mushrooms. Cover and bake in a preheated oven, Gas Mark 6 (200°C/400°F), for about 25 minutes. Remove the cover and bake for a further 5 minutes, adding a little more wine if necessary.

TURKEY WITH LENTILS AND SULTANAS

2 × 125 g (5 oz) turkey breast fillets
1 medium onion, chopped
420 g (15 oz) tin cooked lentils, drained (if using dried, cook as directed)
50 g (2 oz) sultanas
5 ml (1 tsp) chopped fresh mint
juice of 1/2 lemon
freshly ground black pepper and salt
125 g (5 oz) low-fat natural yogurt

Grill the turkey breast fillets under a medium heat for 20–30 minutes or until golden, turning occasionally. Meanwhile, put the chopped onion in a medium pan with a little water, bring to the boil then simmer for about 8 minutes, reducing the liquid to about 15 ml (1 tbsp). Add the lentils, sultanas, mint, lemon juice and freshly ground black pepper, then finally add the yogurt, stirring continuously until heated through.

MOROCCAN TURKEY

2 × 125 g (5 oz) turkey breast
 fillets
10 ml (2 tsp) olive oil
1 medium onion, chopped
15 ml (1 tbsp) chopped fresh
 parsley
3 ml (1/2 tsp) ground
 cinnamon
3 ml (1/2 tsp) ground
 turmeric

paprika, to taste
freshly ground black pepper
juice of 1/2 lemon
420 g (15 oz) tin cooked
 chick peas, drained (if
 using dried, cook as
 directed)
25 g (1 oz) flaked almonds

Grill the turkey breast fillets under a medium heat for 20–30 minutes or until golden, turning occasionally. Meanwhile, heat the olive oil in a pan and cook the onion over a medium heat for 8 minutes, stirring occasionally. Mix together the parsley, cinnamon, turmeric, paprika and black pepper with the lemon juice and 30 ml (2 tbsp) water. Pour over the onion and stir constantly for about 3 minutes, reducing the liquid if necessary. Add the cooked chick peas and the flaked almonds and heat thoroughly. Serve the turkey on individual plates with the sauce poured over. Sprinkle a little paprika on to the turkey.

MEXICAN TURKEY FILLETS

2 × 125 g (5 oz) turkey breast
 fillets
1 medium onion, chopped
420 g (15 oz) tin chopped
 tomatoes
100 g (4 oz) mushrooms,
 sliced
1 medium red pepper, sliced

chilli sauce, to taste
freshly ground black pepper
 and salt
220 g (8 oz) cooked red
 kidney beans
100 g (4 oz) sweetcorn
fresh parsley

Grill the turkey breast fillets under a medium heat for 20–30 minutes or until golden, turning occasionally. Meanwhile, put the onion and chopped tomatoes into a pan and cook over a medium heat for 5 minutes, stirring to prevent sticking. Add the sliced mushrooms, red pepper, chilli sauce to taste, some freshly ground black pepper and salt and cook for a further 5 minutes. Add the cooked red kidney beans and sweetcorn and heat thoroughly. Serve the turkey on individual plates with the vegetables poured over. Garnish with fresh parsley.

VENISON IN RED WINE

300 g (10 oz) venison, cut into bite-size pieces
1 red onion, chopped
1 clove garlic, finely chopped
250 ml (9 fl oz) red wine

5 ml (1 tsp) dried mixed herbs
100 g (4 oz) mushrooms, chopped
5 ml (1 tsp) balsamic vinegar
freshly ground black pepper

Put the venison, onion, garlic, wine and herbs into a casserole, cover, and cook in a preheated oven, Gas Mark 6 (200°C/400°F), for about 1 hour. Add the mushrooms, balsamic vinegar and freshly ground black pepper and cook, uncovered, for a further 15 minutes.

GUINEA FOWL WITH CHESTNUTS

2 guinea fowl breast fillets, skin removed
10–12 chestnuts
10 ml (2 tsp) olive oil
1 clove garlic, finely chopped

125 ml (5 fl oz) white wine
2 bay leaves
100 g (4 oz) mushrooms, chopped
freshly ground black pepper

Make a slit in the shells of the chestnuts and put them on a baking tray. Roast in a preheated oven, Gas Mark 6 (200°C/400°F), for 30 minutes. Allow to cool slightly then peel. Meanwhile, heat the olive oil in a pan and cook the guinea fowl breast fillets for 10 minutes then add the garlic, wine and bay leaves. Cook for a further 15 minutes, turning occasionally to cook evenly. Add the mushrooms, freshly ground black pepper and the chestnuts. Cook, stirring continuously for a few minutes, then serve.

△ Meat

BEEF BOURGUIGNON

300 g (10 oz) lean beef steak, cut into bite-size pieces
1 medium onion, chopped
2 medium carrots, sliced
250 ml (9 fl oz) red wine
100 g (4 oz) mushrooms, chopped

50 g (2 oz) lean bacon, cut into small pieces
5 ml (1 tsp) dried mixed herbs
freshly ground black pepper

Put the beef steak, onion, carrots and red wine into a large pan and cook over a medium heat for about 25 minutes, stirring occasionally. Add the mushrooms, bacon, herbs and black pepper and cook for a further 5 minutes, adding more wine or a little water if necessary.

BEEF TAGINE

300 g (10 oz) lean beef, cut into bite-size pieces
1 red onion, chopped
1 stick celery, chopped
2 medium potatoes, peeled and cut into 2.5 cm (1 inch) cubes
300 ml (10 fl oz) vegetable stock

1 green pepper, cut into strips
125 ml (5 fl oz) red wine
5 ml (1 tsp) balsamic vinegar
chilli sauce, to taste
15 ml (1 tbsp) chopped fresh flat-leaf parsley
freshly ground black pepper

Put the beef, onion, celery, potatoes and vegetable stock into a large ovenproof dish. Cover and cook in a preheated oven, Gas Mark 6 (200°C/400°F), for about 1 hour or until the meat is tender. Add the green pepper, red wine, balsamic vinegar, chilli sauce to taste, parsley and some freshly ground black pepper. Cook uncovered for a further 10 minutes.

ROYAL INDIAN BEEF

300 g (10 oz) lean beef, cut into thin strips
1 medium onion, chopped
10 ml (2 tsp) ground coriander
5 ml (1 tsp) ground cumin
5 ml (1 tsp) ground turmeric
100 g (4 oz) mushrooms, chopped
chilli sauce, to taste
50 g (2 oz) ground almonds
freshly ground black pepper and salt
75 ml (3 fl oz) low-fat single cream
25 g (1 oz) flaked almonds, toasted

Put the beef, onion, coriander, cumin and turmeric into a pan with 300 ml (10 fl oz) water and bring to the boil. Cover and simmer for about 20 minutes or until the meat is tender, stirring occasionally. Reduce the liquid to about 30 ml (2 tbsp). Add the mushrooms, chilli sauce to taste, ground almonds, some freshly ground black pepper and salt and cook for a further 5 minutes. Stir in the cream and heat thoroughly. Serve garnished with toasted almonds.

BEEF BROCHETTES

300 g (10 oz) lean beef steak, cubed
5 ml (1 tsp) olive oil
10 ml (2 tsp) lemon juice
5 ml (1 tsp) mustard
5 ml (1 tsp) dried mixed herbs
freshly ground black pepper
1 red onion, cut into wedges
1 small green pepper, cut into large pieces
1 small red pepper, cut into large pieces
2 medium courgettes, cut into large slices

Mix together the olive oil, lemon juice, mustard, herbs and black pepper and put the cubes of beef steak into this marinade. Leave in the fridge for at least 30 minutes – if possible, for 2 or 3 hours – turning occasionally. Arrange the beef steak on skewers with the onion, green and red peppers and courgettes and cook under a hot grill for about 15 minutes, turning to cook evenly.

ORIENTAL PORK

300 g (10 oz) pork fillet
10 ml (2 tsp) sunflower oil
1 small green pepper, diced
1 small red pepper, diced
small piece root ginger, finely
  shredded

10 ml (2 tsp) Nam Pla fish
  sauce
10 ml (2 tsp) soy sauce
freshly ground black pepper
4 spring onions, shredded

Cut the pork fillet into thin strips. Heat the sunflower oil in a large pan then cook the pork over a medium heat for about 15 minutes, stirring occasionally. Add the green and red peppers, ginger, fish sauce, soy sauce and black pepper and cook for a further 5 minutes. At the last moment, stir in the shredded spring onions.

PORK WITH MEDITERRANEAN VEGETABLES

300 g (10 oz) pork fillet, in
  one piece
10 ml (2 tsp) olive oil
10 ml (2 tsp) lemon juice
1 medium red onion,
  chopped
1 clove garlic, finely chopped
1 small aubergine, chopped

420 g (15 oz) tin chopped
  tomatoes
1 bouquet garni
2 medium courgettes, sliced
1 small red pepper, diced
freshly ground black pepper
2 sprigs fresh parsley

Put the pork fillet into an ovenproof dish with the olive oil and lemon juice. Marinate for 1 hour or longer, if possible. Cover and bake for 30 minutes in a preheated oven, Gas Mark 6 (200°C/400°F). Meanwhile, put the onion, garlic, aubergine, chopped tomatoes and bouquet garni into a large pan and cook over a medium heat for 10 minutes, stirring occasionally to prevent sticking. Add the courgettes, red pepper and some freshly ground black pepper and cook for a further 5 minutes. Remove the bouquet garni. Cut the pork fillet into 2 cm (3/4 inch) round slices. Serve the vegetables with overlapping slices of pork fillet arranged on them. Garnish with sprigs of parsley.

PORK WITH LEMON AND CINNAMON

300 g (10 oz) pork fillet, cut into thin strips
1 medium onion, chopped
1 lemon
10 ml (2 tsp) tomato purée
5 ml (1 tsp) ground coriander
3 ml (1/2 tsp) ground cumin
5 ml (1 tsp) ground cinnamon
freshly ground black pepper and salt
1 small red pepper, chopped
5 ml (1 tsp) chopped fresh coriander

Put the pork fillet and onion into a large saucepan and cover with cold water. Bring to the boil then simmer over a medium heat for about 10 minutes. Cut 2 slices from the lemon and cut into small pieces, then juice the rest of the lemon. Mix the lemon juice with the tomato purée, ground coriander, cumin, cinnamon, black pepper and salt. Reduce the meat juices to about 30 ml (2 tbsp) then stir in the tomato and spice mixture and chopped red pepper. Cook for a further 5 minutes then stir in the lemon pieces and fresh coriander.

LAMB WITH AUBERGINE

300 g (10 oz) lean lamb, minced
1 medium aubergine, cubed
1 red onion, finely chopped
1 clove garlic, finely chopped
300 ml (10 fl oz) tomato passata
1 green pepper, diced
100 g (4 oz) mushrooms, thinly sliced
juice of 1/2 lemon
5 ml (1 tsp) dried mixed herbs
freshly ground black pepper

Put the cubed aubergine into a pan and cover with water. Bring to the boil and simmer for 10 minutes then drain. Meanwhile, put the lamb, onion, garlic and tomato passata into a large pan and cook over a medium heat for 25 minutes. Add the green pepper, mushrooms, lemon juice, herbs, freshly ground black pepper and the aubergine and cook for a further 5 minutes, stirring occasionally.

PERSIAN LAMB

300 g (10 oz) lean lamb,
  cubed
10 ml (2 tsp) olive oil
1 medium onion, chopped
25 g (1 oz) sultanas
strip of orange peel, shredded
3 ml (1/2 tsp) ground
  cinnamon

150 g (6 oz) long-grain rice
1 medium green pepper,
  chopped
freshly ground black pepper
  and salt
25 g (1 oz) flaked almonds,
  toasted

Heat the olive oil in a large pan and cook the onion and the cubed lamb over a medium heat for 10 minutes, stirring to prevent sticking. Add the sultanas, orange peel and ground cinnamon. Add 300 ml (10 fl oz) water, stir thoroughly then cover and simmer for about 30 minutes, stirring occasionally. Meanwhile, cook the rice as directed, drain and keep warm. Add the green pepper, freshly ground black pepper and salt to the lamb, reducing the liquid if necessary. Stir in the rice and amalgamate all ingredients. Serve on individual plates garnished with the toasted almonds.

LAMB WITH APRICOTS

2 × 125 g (5 oz) lean lamb
  steaks
1 medium red onion,
  chopped
1 medium green pepper, cut
  into strips
6 dried apricots, soaked in
  water and chopped

300 ml (10 fl oz) tomato
  passata
chilli sauce, to taste
5 ml (1 tsp) chopped fresh
  mint
freshly ground black pepper
2 sprigs fresh mint, chopped

Grill the lamb steaks under a medium grill for about 15 minutes, turning occasionally to cook evenly. Meanwhile, put the onion and green pepper into a pan with 125 ml (5 fl oz) water and cook over a medium heat for about 8 minutes. Reduce the liquid to about 15 ml (1 tbsp) then add the apricots, tomato passata, chilli sauce to taste, mint and some freshly ground black pepper and heat thoroughly. Serve the lamb steaks on individual plates with the sauce spooned over the meat. Garnish with a sprig of mint.

△ Desserts

SUMMER FRUIT SALAD

8 strawberries, halved	50 g (2 oz) redcurrants
100 g (4 oz) raspberries	icing sugar
100 g (4 oz) blackcurrants	2 sprigs fresh mint

Clean all the fruit. Gently mix together, taking care not to break up the fruit. Serve in individual dishes dusted with icing sugar and garnished with a sprig of mint. This is delicious served with Greek yogurt.

RHUBARB FOOL

4 large stems rhubarb	10 ml (2 tsp) clear honey
15 ml (1 tbsp) freshly squeezed orange juice	125 g (5 oz) low-fat natural yogurt

Cut the ends from the rhubarb and clean it. Cut into 2.5 cm (1 inch) pieces and put in a pan with the orange juice. Cover and cook over a medium heat for about 10 minutes, stirring occasionally to prevent sticking. Add a little more orange juice or some water if necessary. The pieces of rhubarb should break up. Leave to cool then stir in the honey and yogurt and amalgamate all ingredients. Put into individual dishes and chill for at least 30 minutes.

BLUEBERRY COOLER

300 g (10 oz) fresh blueberries	125 g (5 oz) low-fat natural yogurt
	10 ml (2 tsp) clear honey

Mix the yogurt with 5 ml (1 tsp) honey in a bowl then add the blueberries, coating them with the yogurt. Put into individual dishes then chill for at least 30 minutes. Drizzle 5 ml (1 tsp) honey over the blueberry cooler before serving.

EXOTIC FRUIT KEBABS

2 kiwi fruit
1 carambola (star fruit)

wedge of watermelon
1/2 lime

Peel and quarter the kiwi fruit. Cut the carambola into 8 mm (1/3 inch) slices and cut off the skin, keeping the star shape intact. Cut the watermelon from the skin then cut the flesh into pieces about the size of the kiwi fruit quarters. Using 15 cm (6 inch) kebab sticks, arrange the fruit to make 4 kebabs. Serve on individual plates with lime juice squeezed over the kebabs.

MARINATED MELON

1/2 cantaloup melon
100 ml (4 fl oz) dessert wine

redcurrants, or other berries, to garnish

Cut the melon from the skin then cut the flesh into pieces. Put into individual dishes and pour the dessert wine over the melon. Marinate in the refrigerator for at least 30 minutes. At the last moment, garnish with a sprig of redcurrants.

CARIBBEAN FRUIT SALAD

1 small mango
1 small paw paw
1 passion fruit
1 banana

small wedge of pineapple
juice of 1/2 lemon
juice of 1/2 orange

Cut the mango in half, remove the flesh from the skin and cut into pieces. Halve the paw paw, scoop out the seeds and discard them, then remove the flesh from the skin and cut into pieces. Cut the passion fruit in half and scoop out the flesh and seeds. Peel the banana and slice. Cut the flesh from the pineapple wedge and cut into pieces. Mix together all the fruit with the lemon and orange juices then put into individual dishes. Chill before serving.

BUZET PEARS

2 large pears
220 ml (8 fl oz) Buzet or
    other red wine

10 ml (2 tsp) clear honey

Peel the pears. Put them into a small pan with the wine, cover and poach gently for 10–15 minutes. Turn the pears occasionally so that they are evenly coloured by the red wine, adding more wine if necessary. Stir the honey into the wine. Serve either hot or chilled.

WINTER FRUIT SALAD

1 apple
1 pear
1 banana
small bunch of grapes
100 ml (4 fl oz) white wine

3 ml (½ tsp) ground
    cinnamon
2 cloves
5 ml (1 tsp) clear honey

Put the wine in a pan with the ground cinnamon, cloves and honey. Simmer for about 5 minutes then leave to cool. Remove and discard the cloves. Cut the apple, pear and banana into pieces and halve the grapes. Put into a bowl then pour the wine over the fruit. Serve in individual dishes.

STRAWBERRIES IN GRAND MARNIER

220 g (8 oz) strawberries
15 ml (1 tbsp) Grand Marnier

juice of 1/2 orange

Prepare the strawberries and put them in individual dishes. Mix together the Grand Marnier and orange juice and spoon over the strawberries. Marinate in the refrigerator for an hour before serving.

SPICY APRICOTS

6 fresh apricots, halved
125 g (5 oz) low-fat natural
  yogurt
5 ml (1 tsp) ground
  cinnamon

25 g (1 oz) flaked almonds,
  toasted
2 sprigs fresh mint

Mix together the yogurt and half of the cinnamon then coat the apricot halves with this mixture. Put into individual dishes and chill for an hour. Scatter the rest of the cinnamon and the toasted almonds on the apricots. Serve garnished with a sprig of mint.